A WORLD DOWN

Four Essays on the Life and Theology of Martin Luther

Charles E. Fry
Cruciform Press | September 2015

*With love and high esteem for
Jerry Bridges,
The Reverend Bob Barbour,
My father and mother, Charles and Carol Fry,
My parents-in-law, Howard (1932–2009) and Thelma
Thomas, and my dear wife, Lisa, and daughter, Heidi,*

I dedicate this book to God—

*"The blessed and only Sovereign, the King of kings and Lord
of lords, who alone possesses immortality and dwells in
unapproachable light, whom no man has seen or can see. To
him be honor and eternal dominion! Amen."*

(1 Timothy 6:15–16)

CruciformPress

"We are theological hobbits, but we can stand on the shoulders of giants like Martin Luther to get a better view of the glory of Christ and his gospel. Charles Fry has helped us climb onto Luther's shoulders with this little book. It's a wonderful introduction and survey of Luther's life and theology — a book well worth the read."

J. V. Fesko, Academic Dean, Professor of Systematic and Historical Theology, Westminster Seminary California

"Today, the doctrine of justification (that is, being counted as righteous by God through faith in Christ alone), is widely accepted, and at the same time vigorously denied. So we constantly need a reaffirmation and clarification of the gospel as it is taught to us by the apostle Paul and rediscovered by Martin Luther. And Chuck Fry has done an excellent job of summarizing and clarifying for us Luther's understanding of the gospel. There is much in Chuck's book that I could single out as important to Luther's understanding of the gospel, but there is one truth that I especially resonate with. That is Luther's understanding of 'the reality of sin in the life of a Christian and the subsequent need to live daily by the gospel.' My view of the evangelical church today is that the majority of Christians believe we are saved by grace, but we relate to God on the basis of our works. The truth, however, is that our very best deeds on our very best days are still flawed both in motive and performance. As one of the Puritans so aptly said, 'Even my tears of repentance need to be washed in the blood of the Lamb.' So I commend Chuck Fry's book to you. If, by God's grace, you see yourself as a still practicing sinner, this book will encourage you to live by the gospel every day."

Jerry Bridges (from the Foreword), author and speaker

"Luther rediscovered the pure gospel, which radically changed his life and changed the world, from that age to the present. Although the Reformation occurred five centuries ago, the need for reformation continues in our personal and corporate lives. Despite having been an evangelical Christian for decades, in the mid-2000s I found myself in desperate need. Weighed down by law-based living, I carried unnecessary burdens of condemnation and fear that plagued my daily existence. Luther's life and message brought about a gospel-awakening that changed everything for me. The resulting joy impacted my walk, my family, and my vocation. I pray that Chuck Fry's introduction to Luther will help bring the powerful force of the true gospel into the lives of a new generation of believers. The strong, clear articulation of law and gospel in chapter 2 is by itself worth the price of the book. As Luther said, 'Distinguishing between the Law and the gospel is the highest art in Christendom.' May this book stir in you a passion to go further up and further in."

Bill Walsh, Director of International Outreach, The Gospel Coalition

"As one who has fervently believed in justification by faith for many decades, I was humbled and surprised by how desperately I needed to hear it again, and how delightfully encouraging it is to have it enter more deeply into my heart. The clarity and simplicity of these essays, expounding Martin Luther's universally needed message of grace, has the power to lift the weight of condemnation from the soul of both the elite scholar and the simple plow-boy."

C. FitzSimons Allison, retired Episcopal Bishop of South Carolina, author of *The Rise of Moralism and Trust in an Age of Arrogance*

Cruciform**Press**

Books of about 100 pages
Clear, inspiring, gospel-centered

We like to keep it simple. So we publish short, clear, useful, inexpensive books for Christians and other curious people. Books that make sense and are easy to read, even as they tackle serious subjects.

We do this because the good news of Jesus Christ—the gospel—is the only thing that actually explains why this world is so wonderful and so awful all at the same time. Even better, the gospel applies to every single area of life, and offers real answers that aren't available from any other source.

These are books you can afford, enjoy, finish easily, benefit from, and remember. Check us out and see. Then join us as part of a publishing revolution that's good news for the gospel, the church, and the world.

CruciformPress.com

A World Upside Down: Four Essays on the Life and Theology of Martin Luther

Print / PDF ISBN: 978-1-941114-08-7
ePub ISBN: 978-1-941114-10-0
Mobipocket ISBN: 978-1-941114-09-4

Table of Contents

Now we know that whatever the law says, it speaks to those who are under the law, that every mouth may be closed and all the world may become accountable to God; because by the works of the law no flesh shall be justified in his sight; for through the law comes the knowledge of sin. But now apart from the law the righteousness of God has been manifested, being witnessed by the law and the Prophets, even the righteousness of God through faith in Jesus Christ for all those who believe.

Romans 3:19–22

He is not righteous who does much, but he who, without work, believes much in Christ. The law says, 'Do this,' and it is never done. Grace says, 'Believe in this' and everything is already done.

Martin Luther

But God hath chosen the foolish things of the world to confound the wise; and God hath chosen the weak things of the world to confound the things which are mighty; And base things of the world, and things which are despised, hath God chosen, yea, and things which are not, to bring to naught things that are; That no flesh should glory in his presence.

1 Corinthians 1:27–29 (KJV)

Abbreviations

Concord   *The Book of Concord: The Confessions of the Evangelical Lutheran Church*, Robert Kolb and Timothy J. Wengert, eds. (Minneapolis: Fortress Press, 2000)

Galatians   *A Commentary on St. Paul's Epistle to the Galatians*: Based on Lectures Delivered by Martin Luther at the University of Wittenberg in the year 1531 and First Published in 1535, Philip S. Watson (ed.), A revised and completed translation based on the "Middleton" edition of the English version of 1575 (Logos Bible Software)

Sermons   *The Complete Sermons of Martin Luther*, 7 volumes, Eugene F.A. Klug (ed.), Eugene F.A. Klug, Erwin W. Koehlinger, James Lanning, Everette W. Meier, Dorothy Schoknecht, and Allen Schuldheiss, translators (Grand Rapids: Baker Books, 2000)

FOREWORD

By Jerry Bridges

As one who can identify with the words of the apostle Paul, "Christ Jesus came into the world to save sinners, among whom I am foremost of all" (1 Timothy 1:15), I love the gospel. I can't get enough of it. So it was with delight that I read Chuck Fry's manuscript on Martin Luther and the gospel.

God used Martin Luther to rediscover the wonderful truth of justification by faith in Christ alone apart from any works of merit on our part. But this was not simply an intellectual discovery. Rather, it came after some years of vainly seeking to earn heaven by his own efforts. But the more he tried, the more he realized he could never achieve eternal life by himself. And he began to hate God because he thought God had set before him a standard impossible to meet and would then damn him for his failure.

As he studied the Scriptures, however, the Holy Spirit opened the eyes of Luther's understanding so that he came to realize that the righteousness of God which Paul speaks of in Romans 1:17, and again in Romans 3:21–22, is not a righteousness which God requires of us and which we cannot provide. Rather it is a righteousness which

God gives to us, the perfect righteousness of his own Son, Jesus Christ, which we receive through faith. As Luther realized this truth of the gospel, it seemed as if the gates of Paradise opened up to him.

Today, the doctrine of justification (that is, being counted as righteous by God through faith in Christ alone), is widely accepted, and at the same time vigorously denied. So we constantly need a reaffirmation and clarification of the gospel as it is taught to us by the apostle Paul and rediscovered by Martin Luther. And Chuck Fry has done an excellent job of summarizing and clarifying for us Luther's understanding of the gospel.

There is much in Chuck's book that I could single out as important to Luther's understanding of the gospel, but there is one truth that I especially resonate with. That is Luther's understanding of "the reality of sin in the life of a Christian and the subsequent need to live daily by the gospel." My view of the evangelical church today is that the majority of Christians believe we are saved by grace, but we relate to God on the basis of our works. The truth, however, is that our very best deeds on our very best days are still flawed both in motive and performance. As one of the Puritans so aptly said, "Even my tears of repentance need to be washed in the blood of the Lamb."

So I commend Chuck Fry's book to you. If, by God's grace, you see yourself as a still practicing sinner, this book will encourage you to live by the gospel every day.

Jerry Bridges
Colorado Springs, Colorado
Author, *The Pursuit of Holiness*

Introduction
A WORLD UPSIDE DOWN

Shortly before Martin Luther died, a piece of paper bearing his handwriting was found in his pocket. Among other words on the paper were these: "This is true. We are all beggars."[1]

During his lifetime, Luther had come to see the holiness and justice of God. He realized he had no righteousness whatsoever to declare him acceptable to God. Luther only had Christ. Yet, in having Christ, he had everything: assurance of heaven, peace with God, and a calm heart before the Law of God. Simply clinging to Christ alone, Martin Luther inadvertently turned 1500s Europe upside down.

In the fall of 1984, I came to see in a deeper way the truth of Luther's words, "We are all beggars." My pastor preached one day on Matthew 5:3, "Blessed are the poor in spirit, for theirs is the kingdom of heaven." Through this sermon, I was brought face to face with the holiness of God. I was subsequently led to see that I had no righteousness or godliness to give to God in light of his majesty. Yet, in the same sermon, I heard the gospel, the announcement of good news that comes from God himself. Christ the Lord was freely and sweetly offered as a perfect Savior. His once-and-for-all death on the cross was truly sufficient to pay the penalty for all my sin—past, present, and future. I was reminded that I had been justified by faith alone, resting from my own works. As the leaves fell that day in my hometown in Appalachia, heaven once again seemed to come to earth, as the old saying goes. I knew without a doubt that God was my Father in heaven and that I was surrounded by his loving-kindness. I experienced genuine joy.

Almost thirty years later, I taught a class on Martin Luther in the same church where I heard this sermon. In preparing each lecture, I realized how much I personally needed to regularly hear the Law and the gospel clearly proclaimed, as well as the doctrine of justification by faith alone. It is easy to forget, doubt, or trivialize the majesty of God's Law, the grace of God, and the freeness of the gospel announcement. I was struck by the centrality, simplicity, and sufficiency of the gospel for the Church. I also noticed that the gospel is the only message in the world that gives all glory to God and humbles the pride of man. This fact was not missed by Luther. In reading his works, I was struck by his zeal for the glory of God and its connection to the gospel.

In keeping with these observations, I have two goals for this book.

Reformation roots. First, I hope to share concisely with the reader our Reformation roots that have largely been lost. The greatest need of our time is to return to the "first principles" of the Reformation and once again draw straight and simple lines of theology. Studying Martin

Luther is a wonderful way to understand what the Bible teaches concerning God himself, the nature of man, and the gospel. Simply put, I want to share with the reader the wonderful news of the gospel that we may be filled with true joy and peace in believing (Romans 15:13). Martin Luther's need is our need—whether our background is Roman Catholic, Presbyterian, Methodist, Baptist, Lutheran, Anglican, Jewish, atheist, Muslim, Buddhist, Hindu, or anything else. God has clearly spoken in the Bible, telling us that every person in the world is accountable to him and that we are all bankrupt sinners in light of his majesty, holiness, and righteousness (Romans 3:9–20). All of us need the cross of Christ. All of us need a righteousness outside of ourselves that only Jesus can provide. This is our only hope.

Luther's gospel focus. The second goal in writing this book is to show from Luther's work that while the gospel is the only true source of peace and joy, it is also the only message that gives complete glory to God. Certainly, Luther desired for man to receive comfort and hope from the good news of Christ. Yet he was concerned that the Church be faithful to the gospel message so that God would receive all honor. He despised the ways in which man robbed God of his glory; he longed for the medieval church to be humbled before God and to exalt Christ alone.

Overview

Chapter one. The first chapter is a brief biography of Luther's life. To understand Luther's beliefs, it is important to know the context in which he lived and the religion he knew from first-hand experience. This chapter focuses on Luther's life in relationship to the gospel and the religion of merit that was pervasive in his day. Because of this focus, many events of Luther's life are omitted, such as his marriage to Katherine and their six children (one of whom died as an infant and another who died in her teens). While these events are important to study, for the sake of brevity and focus, such aspects of Luther's story are not found in this narrative.

Chapter two. The second chapter discusses Luther's understanding of the gospel. Key to Luther's thought is a proper distinction between the Law and the gospel. In our day this distinction is typically trivialized, psychologized, blurred, or extinguished altogether. Thus the gospel is lost. Yet to Luther, distinguishing between the two allowed one to face God and his Word in all its infinite holiness and, therefore, to be genuinely contrite, resting in the finished work of Christ. This clarification leads one to the doctrine of justification by faith alone, which Luther understood as being the core of the gospel.

Justification by faith alone is the biblical truth that a person is declared spotless and righteous by God himself through reliance on Jesus Christ alone for forgiveness and salvation. In being justified, all our sins are freely pardoned and we are clothed in the perfect obedience of Christ. Justification was the end of all that Luther taught. Along with the Law/gospel distinction and justification by faith alone, this chapter also discusses other essential issues related to the gospel, such as Luther's teaching on repentance and faith, the will of man, and the reality of sin in the believer's life.

Chapter three. The third chapter discusses the way in which Martin Luther's understanding of the gospel exalts God and humbles man. While the material in this section may be the least familiar to the reader, Luther's teaching on this subject was remarkably helpful and should be treasured. Luther's zeal to connect the gospel with the glory of God was second to none.

This chapter will consider Luther's *Heidelberg Disputation*, where we see his theology of glory and his theology of the cross. Luther's classic work, *The Freedom of the Christian,* is also examined, along with a few other select writings. Here Luther notes that the only person in the world who is able to produce genuine fruit for the glory of God is the person who rests in the finished work of Christ. He longed for the Church to produce fruit for the glory of God. However, he simply wanted good works to be in their proper place—completely apart from one's standing before God (which is based on Christ's work alone), a happy result of being freely declared righteous by God.

Chapter four. The final chapter, *Christ's Church*, seeks to summarize the message of the preceding chapters and apply this message to our lives in the twenty-first century. Though this is the shortest chapter, it is perhaps the most important.

Appendix. Lastly, in the Appendix a simplified timeline is presented of the main events and writings of Luther's life as discussed in this book. This will help the reader more clearly understand how the details of Luther's life fit into his overarching story and that of the Reformation.

In his preface to *The Complete Sermons on Martin Luther,* Eugene F.A. Klug observes,

Many excellent biographies of [Luther's] life have appeared through the years; but the definitive statement of his theological impact and production has yet to be written, and probably never will, whether by friend or foe. The field is simply too vast, even though Luther was and remained very clear and uncomplicated in every utterance and situation.[2]

I agree with Klug. Luther's life, theology, and impact are so enormous that in the process of writing on him or his theology, one is overwhelmed at the start. Who is adequate for such a task? Yet I find myself also agreeing with Klug when he says that Luther is "clear and uncomplicated." The doctrine of justification by faith alone is the unifying thread throughout his works and sermons. Indeed, Luther himself described faith in Christ as his entire theology: "For the one doctrine which I have supremely at heart, is that of faith in Christ, from whom, through whom, and unto whom all my theological thinking flows back and forth day and night."[3]

Thus, we can have reasonable assurance that we are interpreting Martin Luther correctly, for he did have this one unifying theme to his work—and what a glorious, life-giving theme it is.

On a Friday afternoon outside Jerusalem nearly two thousand years ago, our Savior—one hundred percent God, one hundred percent man—hung on a cross. As others have noted, had we been there and been close enough to that awful event, we would have heard the sound of flies. Blood would have fallen on our hands as we touched splintered wood. We would have heard dry, anguished gasps escape from our Lord's swollen throat as his life came to an end. We would have seen Christ buried. And three days later, we would have seen an empty tomb. Christ's death and resurrection for our sins is an objective fact of history which remains, for all times and cultures, an unchanged comfort for guilty consciences.

Either Jesus' death for all our sins is enough or it is not. If Christ is enough (and he is), then it is folly to trust our own works or to try to add one atom of righteousness to Christ's work. There is no middle ground, no mixture of his work plus our work. There is only pure and unchanging grace for the child of God, where Christ alone is the anchor of our souls (Hebrews 6:19, 20). If we do not believe that Christ is enough, then our faith crumbles to nothing.

Martin Luther found the life, death, and resurrection of Jesus Christ to be more than enough. As Luther clung to Christ alone, the world was turned upside down. May the whole world, like Luther, know and trust the gospel of God, and in trusting, find true rest.

One
WHEN LIGHTNING STRUCK

A Brief Life of Martin Luther

The wicked flee when no one is pursuing,
But the righteous are bold as a lion.

Proverbs 28:1

On January 12, 1519, the Emperor of the Holy Roman Empire, Maximilian I, came to the end of his days and his earthly power. To prepare for the life to come, he gave orders for "his body to be scourged, his hair shorn, his teeth broken out,"[4] hoping to appear before God as a penitent. Such instructions revealed the religious thought of his day: man was guilty before God, but if he could demonstrate through suffering, sacrifice, and acts of penance that he was remorseful enough over his sin and earnest in giving God something of his own merit, he might fare better in the afterlife. Such was the religion that dripped from a medieval and Renaissance Europe saturated with fear and religious superstition. It was in this atmosphere that Martin Luther lived his days. In order to understand Luther, it is important to first consider the context in which he lived, particularly this merit-based religion that permeated society.

The Renaissance and Medieval Christianity

Most would agree that the Renaissance began around the mid-1300s in Italy and ended in the mid-1500s. Though the period contained much fear and superstition, it was also a time of great achievement, discovery, and change. The word "Renaissance" itself is French for "rebirth," and during this time there were indeed significant changes in the arts, politics, exploration, and approaches to theology. Along with these came the invention of the printing press (circa 1400–1450), a rediscovery of the literary classics, and a renewed focus on the ancient sources, a movement later referred to as humanism. The cry of Renaissance humanism was *ad fontes*, "back to the sources." With this focus came a renewed emphasis on the Bible and biblical languages, and a re-examining of all that was once assumed to be true.

The Renaissance came as an explosion in Italy, affecting every area of culture and the life of the church, and giving a unique shape to society. While the Renaissance brought great pride in the glory of man's attainments, and optimism about the direction of the world, it also engendered great uncertainty about the eternal destiny of one's life, this being a fruit of medieval Christianity. Lewis Spitz captures the paradox of the Renaissance age:

> [It] was an age of powerful personalities, cruel
> military men, clever and ruthless statesmen, but
> also of exquisite artists, gentle poets, and dedicated
> scholars. There were men of enormous wealth, but
> multitudes who suffered abject poverty. It was a
> time when nights were consumed in debauchery, but
> also devoted to vigils and prayer. It was a time for
> display and pomp, but also for preachers of penitence,
> humility, and withdrawal to solitary life. It was a day
> for progress coupled with retrogression. It boasted
> of the dignity of man but bewailed his misery. It
> could be humanistic and yet act totally inhumane.
> It coupled a pronounced interest in man with a
> weariness with life and a longing for a celestial home.[5]

Though the Renaissance came rapidly to Italy, it took
root more slowly in its neighbor to the north, Germany.[6]
Renaissance thought would eventually make inroads
into Germany, affecting its education and theology, but
in Luther's day German culture was still dominated by a
medieval religion of fear and superstition. For instance,
Frederick the Wise, who ruled over Saxony in Germany,
boasted of a personal collection of 5005 relics, whereby
he could erase 1,443 years of purgatory for the "adoring
faithful." His prized collection was purported to include
four hairs from Mary's head, a piece of straw from Jesus'
manger, a strand of Jesus' beard, and a twig from Moses'
burning bush.[7] Frederick's collection of relics demonstrates the superstitious thinking found in the Germany of
Luther's day.[8] Along with relics came teachings on indulgences and purgatory. The Roman Church taught that
buying an indulgence from the papacy could free one from

the torments of purgatory, a place where the dead pay the penalty for their sins not sufficiently atoned for while living.

The papacy, based in Rome, was also morally corrupt. Pope Innocent VIII, for example, openly celebrated the fact that he had fathered 16 illegitimate children. The father of Pope Leo X, who ruled the Roman Church during the early Reformation, pleaded with his son as he went to Rome to remain pure, calling it the sink of all sins. Early in his career, Luther himself went to Rome and was appalled at the debauchery he found among the priests. Such corruption inevitably influenced the Catholic priesthood in Germany, as well.

A scholarly monastic group, The Brethren of the Common Life, was also present in Germany at this time. While the group was sincere in its devotion to God, it was at the same time mystical in its view of the Christian life. The mystics varied in their theology, but a common thread through their doctrine was salvation by surrender. If you could only surrender enough, they taught, you could jump the chasm formed by sin and reach new heights in your love for and relationship with God.

This was a not-so-subtle form of perfectionism. Several influential writings, including *The Imitation of Christ,* a devotional by Thomas A' Kempis (1380–1471), emerged from the group, giving voice to this mystical and perfectionistic view of Christianity. Another example was *The Way of Perfection,* a book written after Luther's time by Teresa of Avila. Such books discussed valid and important truths such as the humility of Christ, yet the emphasis was not on Christ's work for sinners, but on how people should live. Under such mystical teaching (still common today), one could never know if he or she had surrendered enough to be pleasing to God. Indeed, you would be left to wonder how much could *ever* be enough. Objective faith in Jesus Christ's person and work had given way to the instability of subjective religious experience.

Thus, medieval and Renaissance Germany was indeed a world of lofty ambition concerning its view of man, yet also a world of fear, superstition, purgatory, penance, indulgences, and introspective efforts to justify oneself before God by works. In short, it was a world that did not know grace. This was the world into which Martin Luther was born.

Early Years

Martin Luther was born on November 10, 1483 in Eisleben, Germany. This would also be the place of his death after a life of unexpected turbulence and joy — a life that would turn the world upside down with the announcement of the good news of God's gospel.

He was born to Hans and Margaretta Luther. Like the times in which Martin was born, his parents, by today's standards, were rough, harsh, and stern. Yet they were also religious to a degree and wanted the best for their son. Hans, a copper miner, sacrificed greatly to earn enough money for Martin to study law, the profession of choice and prestige. In 1505, Hans' dream came true: Luther began his study of law at the University of Erfurt.

Lightning

The dream would not last long. On July 2 of his first year at Erfurt, a bolt of lightning knocked Luther to the ground as he returned to school following a visit to his home in Mansfeld. His conscience had already been greatly troubling him with the sense that he was not right with God, nor good enough to be accepted by a holy God. He would later write that the soul whose conscience is sensitive, yet dirty and guilty before the justice of God, is driven by fear to the point where the rustling of a leaf would put one to flight. As Proverbs 28:1 notes, "The wicked flee when no one is pursuing."

It is not hard to imagine, then, the terror that Luther felt from the wrath of God when he was struck by heaven on that hot July day. In response, Luther did the only thing he knew to do. He cried out for a mediator between himself and God, promising good works and self-denial if only he might find a refuge. Specifically, he called out to the patron saint of miners, crying, "Saint Anne, help me! I will become a monk."

In that one cry we can see two of the false beliefs Luther held at that time.

The need for a human mediator. First, the cry suggested that one could not directly approach God without the aid of a created being, such as Mary or Saint Anne—the mediatorial work of Christ on its own was not sufficient to bring one before God. Help was not to be found in the God-man alone as the perfect Savior who gave unmerited favor (grace) to the undeserving and sinful. Rather, a mediator needed to be found even in approaching Christ (the true mediator; cf. 1 Timothy 2:5).

The need for salvation by works. Secondly, we see in Luther's cry his belief that perfect sacrifice and a complete denial of self were needed to assuage the wrath of God.

Luther, of course, promptly kept his word. Fifteen days after the lightning incident he entered the Augustinian order to begin his life as a monk, hoping to earn eternal life by keeping the Law of God. His decision to leave his legal studies infuriated his father, but he was willing to suffer that fury in hopes of calming the wrath of God in heaven.

Luther worked with all his might, plunging himself into the religion of merit, where eternal life was granted to those who earned it. So severe were his personal practices that at times the other monks had to keep him from physical harm, lest he literally kill himself with his religion and penitential strivings.

Doctrinally, this religion of merit was formulated for monks in what was called, "the monastic absolution." This prayer of absolution concisely expressed the system under which Luther labored:

> God forgive thee, my brother. The merit of the passion of our Lord Jesus Christ, and of blessed S. Mary, always a virgin, and of all the saints: the merit of thine order, the straitness of thy religion, the humility of thy confession, the contrition of thy heart, the good works which thou hast done and shalt do for the love of our Lord Jesus Christ, be unto thee available for the remission of thy sins, the increase of merit and grace, and the reward of everlasting life. Amen.[9]

In this prayer, one can clearly see the Roman Church's teaching of gaining forgiveness by offering to God humility, good works, and love for Jesus. If one drew strength and "merit" from the treasury of the accomplished godliness of Mary, Christ, and the saints, and in so doing, lived a holy life, then one would be forgiven. This search for absolution did include a measure of faith in

Christ, yet by itself that faith meant nothing: in order to be effective it had to be paired with one's most severe efforts. This is what almost drove Luther to insanity; he knew he could never do these things well enough, even with the saints' supposed merits to aid him. He could never have a good enough heart before a righteous and just God.

Luther's First Mass

In 1507, Martin Luther conducted his first Mass. This may seem to be of little importance unless we are familiar with the theology behind the sacrament of the Lord's Supper that Luther embraced. The day of Luther's first Mass was supposed to be one of joy, success, and achievement. He was finally a priest and, as such, supposedly vested with power to change the bread and wine into *the literal body and blood of Christ* by a process the Roman Church calls transubstantiation. Luther's father, now somewhat reconciled to his son's vocation, attended the event, signifying a blessing on Luther's life.

What was intended to be a day of joy, however, soon became a day of fear, anxiety, and failure. The moment Luther lifted the bread, believing it had just changed into the actual body and blood of Christ, he trembled, fumbled, and faltered. His fear and trembling before a holy God were so great that he was unable to serve the Lord's Supper properly. Luther was humiliated, and his father left the Mass in disgust, curtly reminding his son of the scriptural injunction to honor his father and mother.

Move to Wittenberg

After four more years of a battered conscience and endless hours of confession to Johann von Staupitz (Luther's spiritual father and mentor), Martin Luther was transferred to the University of Wittenberg to teach theology and the Bible. This was a young but upcoming school, established by the Duke of Saxony (Frederick the Wise, he of the thousands of supposed relics), with the intent of forming one of the strongest universities of his day. Staupitz had Luther transferred there in the hope that he could look outside of himself by academic study and thus find relief from his morbid introspection and anguished conscience. Stauptiz also needed Luther's help in teaching and carrying the academic workload.

Providentially, this move to Wittenberg would be the final event that God would use to bring Luther to the gospel of grace. From 1513 to 1516, Luther lectured at Wittenberg on the Psalms, Romans, and Galatians. This study of God's Word—over against the word of popes, councils, tradition, and the wisdom of the world—would give assurance and comfort to Martin Luther. These convictions, and his increasing understanding of God's Word, would give him courage to stand for Christ against the entire world.

Luther and the Gospel: Peace with God

The entire time that Luther sought to please God through his own actions, he was conscious of the fact that he actually hated the righteousness and justice of God, for they require perfect obedience to the Law of God. He knew that even his best performance could never measure up—despite fasting, sacrificing, trying to fully surrender to God (the mystic way), and confessing his sins to Staupitz for up to six hours at a time. Luther said of this time in his life, "I was myself driven to the very abyss of despair so that I wished I had never been created. Love God? I hated him!"[10]

As he studied the Scriptures at Wittenberg, however, Luther increasingly clung to "the dear Paul," as he put it, for in the apostle's letters Luther began to hear a new and sweet sound: the message of grace. The message of a Savior who had obeyed the Law perfectly on man's behalf and died on the cross, bearing the complete penalty for sin. Luther began to see that the righteousness God required from him was freely given through faith alone. Romans 1:16–17 was the key passage that caused the doors of paradise to open for Luther: "For I am not ashamed of the gospel, for it is the power of God for salvation to everyone who believes, to the Jew first and also to the Greek. For in it the righteousness of God is revealed from faith to faith; as it is written, 'But the righteous man shall live by faith.'"

> At last, meditating day and night and by the mercy of God, I gave heed to the context of the words, "In it the righteousness of God is revealed, as it is written, 'He who through faith is righteous shall live.'" Then I began to understand that the righteousness of God is that through which the righteous live by a gift of God, namely by faith… Here I felt as if I were entirely born again and had entered paradise itself through gates that had been flung open. An entirely new side of the Scriptures opened itself to me… and I extolled my sweetest word with a love as great as the loathing with which before I had hated the term, "the righteousness of God." Thus, that verse in Paul was for me truly the gate of paradise.[11]

God was no longer an angry tyrant who could not be pleased. Instead, through simple trust in the Savior, God had become Luther's kind and compassionate Father:

> If you have a true faith that Christ is your Saviour, then at once you have a gracious God, for faith leads you in and opens up God's heart and will, that you should see pure grace and overflowing love. *This is to behold God in faith that you should look upon his fatherly, friendly heart, in which there is no anger nor ungraciousness.* He who sees God as angry does not see him rightly but looks only on a curtain, as if a dark cloud had been drawn across his face.[12]

Scholars differ as to exactly when Martin Luther came to trust Christ alone for salvation. According to one view, Luther gained a clear understanding of God's grace as early as 1516, roughly a year before he would nail his celebrated 95 Theses to the door of the Wittenberg Church.[13] One piece of evidence for this date comes from a letter Luther wrote that year to a friar named Spenlein, urging the monk to despair of his own righteousness and to trust Christ alone, thus finding all of his righteousness in the Savior.

Although Luther did appear to have some clarity on the gospel in 1516, his 95 Theses, written a year later, are actually not clear at all on the doctrine of justification. In fact, they still seem quite Roman Catholic. One ought not to consult that document to be edified in the riches of grace. In 1518, however, Luther presented The *Heidelberg Disputation*,[14] a major work and one much clearer on the gospel. Nevertheless, some scholars believe it was even later that Luther came to true faith in Christ.

While it seems we cannot know for certain when Luther actually became a Christian, two things are plain. First, Luther's understanding of the Bible's teaching on the gospel of grace did not occur in an instant, but was gradual. Secondly, Luther surely did come to trust Christ alone for salvation. Indeed, for the rest of his life, he would remain faithful to the gospel of God. Armed with assurance of his own righteousness before God, the one whose conscience once trembled at a leaf was now able to stand against the powers of the world, exemplifying the second part of Proverbs 28:1, "The righteous are as bold as a lion."

Peace with God, War with the World

During the period 1513–1516, Luther was lecturing through Paul's epistles and the Psalms and beginning to understand the gospel. Meanwhile, in Rome, Pope Leo X was continuing to build Saint Peter's Cathedral, a project begun in 1506 by Pope Julius II. To help fund that work, a priest named Johann Tetzel was in Germany selling indulgences. For the right price, a person could buy an indulgence that would supposedly guarantee that the purchaser would go to heaven, skipping purgatory entirely. Optionally, the purchase could be used to release a presently tormented soul out of purgatory.

When Luther became aware of Tetzel's practice, he was furious. One result of his outrage was his 95 Theses, which carry the formal title, "Disputation on the Power and Efficacy of Indulgences." Reading this document, it's clear that Luther still believed in purgatory and found some value in indulgences. He was essentially respectful of the Pope and the authority of the Roman Church. He simply thought that Tetzel's methods were trivializing the grace and forgiveness that a "proper" use of indulgences was supposed to produce. He saw Tetzel's approach as the abuse of a valid doctrine by Rome for financial gain.

Thus, by nailing that document to the door of the Wittenberg Church on October 31, 1517, Luther merely intended to promote debate within the Roman Church, as a supportive follower of the Roman Church. He had no idea that in short order his theses would be widely reproduced by the relatively new printing press and distributed to a Germany that was outraged by the oppression and financial tyranny of Rome. Virtually overnight, the Reformation had begun. At the time, no one could imagine the theological breadth it would eventually encompass, going far beyond indulgences to the heart of salvation itself.

The Gospel Becoming Clarified

In 1518, Luther was asked to give a disputation to a group of fellow Augustinian monks in Heidelberg, Germany. This meeting was something of a local gathering where monks and church leaders met to discuss a topic of theology. In this meeting, Luther clarified and expanded more fully what he understood the Scriptures to teach. He sharply opposed the Aristotelian use of reason found in scholastic theology, a practice that left man and his speculative thinking, rather than God's pronouncements, as the final arbiter of truth.

At the core of this disputation, however, Luther presented his contrast between the theology of glory and the theology of the cross. The first might be called a theology of human glory, for it teaches that one can climb to God by worldly thought and reason. By contrast, a theology of the cross is not man-centered but God-centered, embracing the wisdom of God—found chiefly in Christ crucified—as the way to God.

In this theology of the cross, man is absolutely dependent on God for a righteousness outside of himself. Christ did it all; man does nothing but believe. These were Luther's clearest statements up to that time on the gospel and the errors of Rome's theology. This teaching went against the reason of the world and struck at the heart of Roman doctrine. Surprisingly, the Heidelberg Disputation produced little immediate opposition or objection.

Debate and Dispute

Within a year, however, controversy over Luther's teachings had become quite pitched. Luther had gained popularity and notoriety, and had become an annoying fly in the ointment of Rome's religion. From July 4–14, 1519, Luther engaged in a debate over his teachings with John Eck, whom Luther described as a man with "a butcher's face and a bull's voice…[a man] of prodigious memory, torrential fluency, and uncanny acumen." The debate was to take place in Leipzig, some 45 miles from Wittenberg.

About a century earlier another man, John Hus, had become popular for challenging Rome. The Church promised him safe passage to defend his teaching, but the promise was broken and Hus was burned at the stake as a heretic. Aware of the danger of his position, Luther traveled to Leipzig under the protection of two hundred men armed with battle axes; Eck himself was protected by seventy-six bodyguards.[15]

During this debate over the legitimacy of the papacy and various points of doctrine, including the nature of man, Eck quoted the Church fathers, while Luther repeatedly went back to the Scriptures as his final defense and authority. This debate thus helped crystallize for Luther his belief in the doctrine of *sola scriptura* (Scripture alone). Scripture alone is man's final authority—not popes or councils or the traditions of men. Luther stated, "I am bound, not only to assert, but to defend the truth with my blood and death. I want to believe freely and be a slave of no one, whether council, university, or pope. I will confidently confess what appears to me to be true, whether it has been asserted by a Catholic or a heretic."[16]

By 1520, Luther's once-respectful manner of writing to and about the pope had become bold, bitter, and caustic. Pope Leo X, responding in kind, gave this famous and furious prayer against Luther while hunting: "Arise, O Lord, and judge thy cause. A wild boar has invaded thy vineyard." Leo also called on Peter, Paul, and the saints to defend the Church against Luther's "heresies," and issued a papal bull (an official letter), giving Martin Luther sixty days to recant his views. When Luther received the bull, he tossed it in the fire.

In April of the following year, Luther was ordered to the Diet of Worms, a meeting in the German city of Worms consisting of top leaders of the Roman Church. Rome's intention was that Luther would publicly recant his teachings and be brought back into the Church's favor. Despite the dangers of even traveling to this event, Luther chose to go, accepting the passage provided by Rome. As Luther entered the city, it seemed to him as though there were devils on every rooftop. He was preparing to stand against the entire Church, the Holy Roman Empire, and the very hosts of hell.

During the Diet, Luther was asked if he would recant his teaching. Fearful, yet desiring to stand on the side of God and his Word, he asked for a day to think about his answer. After a long night of anguish and prayer, he returned the next day strengthened with the certainty that he was standing with the Word of God. When asked again if he would recant, he gave his famous reply:

> Since then Your Majesty and your lordships desire a simple reply, I will answer without horns and without teeth. Unless I am convicted by Scripture and plain reason—I do not accept the authority of popes and councils, for they have often contradicted each other—my conscience is captive to the Word of God. I cannot and will not recant of anything, for to go against conscience is neither right nor safe. God help me. Amen.[17]

Luther's stand that April day in 1521 would forever change the world. Eugene Klug captures something of the impact of that day on world history:

> It is impossible to proceed very far without at some point feeling the impact of Luther's person upon human history since 1521. His stand at the Diet of Worms in April of that year has, with good reason, been judged to be the continental divide of modern world history. His is a giant presence, like a sky-scraper, inspiring awe the closer one stands or tries to embrace its totality, but most profitably appreci-

ated when viewed from a distance as it provides the bearing point for all else on the horizon.[18]

Luther found peace with God through being justified by faith alone. Yet in finding peace, he discovered he was at war with the world. The irony—that the sweet and pure good news from heaven would bring such enormous warfare and destruction—was not missed by Luther. In his later years, he would reflect on how the world has ever been at war with the gospel, going back even to Paradise and the murder of Abel by Cain. He perceived this rage against the promise of grace continuing on through history, up to his own time. "Yet I am compelled to forget my shame and be quite shameless in view of the horrible profanation and abomination which have always raged in the Church of God, and still rage to-day, against this one solid rock which we call the doctrine of justification." [19]

"I Let the Word Do Its Work"

After leaving Worms to return to Wittenberg, Luther was kidnapped under a ruse by his friends and taken to a German castle called the Wartburg.

Hidden away in the Wartburg, Luther could not be found by a Roman Church that was likely inclined to kill him for his very public and uncompromising stand on God's Word. It also gave him an ideal opportunity to begin translating the Bible into German, something that had never before been done. Church historian Philip Schaff notes the importance of Luther's translation:

> The richest fruit of Luther's leisure in the Wartburg, and the most important and useful work of his

whole life, is the translation of the New Testament,
by which he brought the teaching and example of
Christ and the Apostles to the mind and heart of the
Germans in life-like reproduction. It was a republi-
cation of the gospel. He made the Bible the people's
book in church, school, and house. If he had done
nothing else, he would be one of the greatest benefac-
tors of the German-speaking race.[20]

While Luther was in hiding, his colleague, Andreas
Karlstadt, took it upon himself to direct the Reformation.
He called for radical reforms, as well as the destruction of
any icons or images used as objects of veneration, along
with all things associated with the papacy. After Luther
came out of hiding, he condemned Karlstadt for his
leadership errors and brought stability to the work of the
Reformation.

Much like our day, Luther soon realized the people of
Germany had lived their entire lives ensconced in a merit-
based religion loaded down with extra-biblical teaching
which obscured the general teaching of God's Word.
He was shocked that a people with so much religious
fervor could have little or no basic Bible knowledge.
After visiting Saxony, he noted that professing German
believers typically had no knowledge of God's Word or
basic doctrine, not even knowing the Lord's Prayer or
the Ten Commandments. Even their pastors lacked such
knowledge and were thus unable to teach biblical truth.

The Small Catechism. In response, Luther wrote
what he considered to be one of his two most significant
works, *The Small Catechism* (the other work being, *On
the Bondage of the Will*). Presented in short question-

and-answer format, the *Catechism* set forth a summary of Christian truth even children could absorb. Completed in 1529, it covered the Ten Commandments, the Apostles Creed, the Lord's Prayer, baptism, confession, the Lord's Supper, and ways the head of a Christian family should lead his household.

As Robert Kolb observes, Luther was concerned about two things: telling the overarching story of Scripture (the gospel of God redeeming a people through Christ), and the change that would take place among believers through simple but biblical teaching and preaching. A mere two years after writing the *Catechism*, Luther reflected back on the power of the Word, and specifically the Word taught through the *Catechism*: "It has, praise God, come to this, that men and women, young and old, know the catechism and how to believe, live, pray, suffer, and die."[21]

For the remainder of his life, Luther encountered opposition from two distinct religious camps. One was the Roman Catholic Church with its religion of merit. The other was the Anabaptists. Although the Anabaptists rejected the Roman Catholic view of the authority of tradition, as well as the doctrines of purgatory, indulgences, and more, both Rome and the Anabaptists opposed the Reformation's understanding of the nature and sufficiency of God's holy Word, and thus both movements were enemies of Luther himself.

By this time it was perfectly clear to Luther that the heart of all his concerns came down to the sufficiency of Scripture: sola scriptura—that Scripture alone is the final authority over believers, councils, tradition, and the papacy. By contrast, the Catholic Church placed tradition on equal footing with the Scriptures. Luther realized that this ultimately moved tradition and the Church to a position of authority over the Scriptures. Thus, while Rome taught that the Church determined which books were Scripture, Luther taught that the Scriptures created the Church. With tradition and papal authority as supreme, Rome sought to add to the Scriptures and to the gospel of grace, particularly adding works to the doctrine of justification by faith.

On the Bondage of the Will. As he had done at Heidelberg, Luther also continued to confront the Church's use of an Aristotelian approach to theology, which only further exalted man's reason above the Scriptures. In his characteristically blunt and colorful language, Luther called such reason "the devil's whore," for it set man up as lord over Scripture, rather than allow man to humbly accept what the Scripture taught, regardless of how it may confront one's thinking.

To address this error directly, Luther wrote *On the Bondage of the Will*, focusing especially on *Diatribe*, a book by a Dutch Catholic priest named Erasmus. Erasmus believed the Church's hierarchy had authority over the truth; Luther contended that truth has authority over the Church. Erasmus argued that one should pursue peace in the Church more than truth; Luther taught that truth is lord over peace and often brings division. Erasmus taught that tradition had authority over the Scripture; Luther taught tradition must submit to Scripture.

Throughout Luther's disputes with the Church, issues of political power were always part of the picture, but the real battle was over the sufficiency and authority of God's Word. To the end of his life, Luther battled the Roman Church's view of Scripture.

The Anabaptists. Despite his many concerns with the Roman Church, Luther considered a smaller yet growing theological opponent, the Anabaptists, to be more formidable. This group took the Reformation as their starting point, but then went to a radical end in hopes of regaining what they considered to be pure religion. They heartily embraced extra-biblical revelation, trusting in new revelations supposedly from God, rather than resting in the Bible and hearing God speak through the Scriptures alone.

As a result, the Anabaptists plunged themselves into religious excess and disgrace, wreaking havoc and disruption. Sadly, the papacy and the emperor associated Luther with the Anabaptists and their folly. Therefore, Luther zealously attacked the Anabaptist theology. With respect to both Rome and the Anabaptists, the chief battle was ultimately over the same issue: the doctrine of sola scriptura: Scripture alone.

How did Luther battle any and all enemies of the Reformation? He taught and proclaimed the Word of God, a fact that remains as one of his greatest legacies. Yet Luther's legacy is really God's legacy, for the Holy Spirit used the written and preached Word to bring the Reformation to Europe, which in turn brought the triumph of the gospel once again to the world. Luther expressed his view of the gospel's success:

> I simply taught, preached, and wrote God's Word; otherwise I did nothing. And while I slept [cf. Mark 4:26–29], or drank Wittenberg beer with my friends Philipp and Amsdorf, the Word so greatly weakened the papacy that no prince or emperor ever inflicted

such losses upon it. I did nothing; the Word did everything. Had I desired to foment trouble, I could have brought great bloodshed upon Germany; indeed, I could have started such a game that even the emperor would not have been safe. But what would it have been? Mere fool's play. I did nothing; I let the Word do its work. What do you suppose is Satan's thought when one tries to do the thing by kicking up a row? He sits back in hell and thinks: Oh, what a fine game the poor fools are up to now! But when we spread the Word alone and let it alone do the work, that distresses him. For it is almighty, and takes captive the hearts, and when the hearts are captured the work will fall of itself.[22]

Luther's Death, Luther's Hope

On Christmas afternoon, 1530, Martin Luther preached on Luke 2:1–14 and the hope a Christian has in death because of the child who was born in Bethlehem. He reflected on the time when he would one day die and how nothing in God's creation would be able to help him on that day—except for the baby born in Bethlehem. Only the Savior could be his help and refuge:

> Sun, moon, stars, all creatures, physicians, emperors, kings, wise men and potentates cannot help me. When I die I shall see nothing but black darkness, and yet that light, "To you is born this day the Savior" [Luke 2:11], remains in my eyes and fills all heaven and earth. The Savior will help me when all have forsaken me. And when the heavens and the stars and all creatures stare at me with horrible mien, I see nothing in heaven and earth but this child.[23]

Some sixteen years later, this moment of Luther's life on which he reflected that Christmas day would come to pass. As he lay dying, he continually repeated the promise, "For God so loved the world, that he gave his only begotten Son, that whoever believes in him shall not perish, but have eternal life." On February 18, 1546, Martin Luther died of a ruptured heart in Eisleben, Germany, the very town where his life began. Shortly before his death, Luther was asked to confess one last time the faith for which he had given his life. "Reverend father, will you die steadfast in Christ and the doctrines you have preached?" "Yes," was Luther's simple reply. The world was watching to see if his understanding of the gospel would carry him in the moment of death. In other words, was the gospel of justification by faith alone true? Was it sufficient? Oberman observes that much was at stake in this confession:

> For in the late Middle Ages, ever since the first struggle for survival during the persecutions of ancient Rome, going to one's death with fearless fortitude was the outward sign of a true child of God, of the confessors and martyrs. The deathbed in the Eisleben inn had become a stage; and straining their ears to catch Luther's last words were enemies as well as friends.[24]

Oberman also notes that at Luther's death, there was no "Elisha" who would receive the mantle of the Reformation: "It was not carelessness or self-complacency that had kept Luther from planning for a future without him; instead he was convinced that the power of the rediscovered gospel would be strong enough to make its own way, even in the turmoil he often predicted would follow his death."[25]

Would Luther's confidence in the gospel prove correct? At first it seemed the answer was no. After he died, whole regions of Germany fell to the political and military machinery of the papacy and Emperor Charles V. Through the military victories of Charles, Luther's theology became outlawed and Luther's teachings were forbidden in many areas. The Reformation in Germany seemed to be gasping for breath as the Roman Catholic Church regained strongholds.

In the end, however, Luther was proved correct concerning his confidence in the gospel and his certainty of bright days ahead. The Protestant faith quickly regained strength and spread throughout Europe and the world, changing entire nations. Luther's confidence rested on a firm foundation, for the gospel is truly the power of God for the salvation of everyone who believes. It is the weapon of almighty God and his one essential message for the world. This message that Luther so treasured humbles mankind and gives all glory to God, while at the same time cleansing a guilty conscience and giving assurance and abiding joy to the lowliest of men. The gospel of Christ caused this trembling man to become as bold as a lion.

Luther's understanding of the gospel is much needed again in our day. It will give great joy, freedom, and assurance to us in the twenty-first century. This understanding of the gospel is the focus of the following chapter.

Two

LUTHER'S UNDERSTANDING OF THE GOSPEL

Five Crucial Insights

I do not nullify the grace of God,
for if righteousness comes through the law,
then Christ died needlessly.

Galatians 2:21

In the year 1496, a boy of around 14 years of age observed a startling sight: a prince named William of Anhalt walking the streets of Magdeburg, Germany, emaciated and begging, carrying a sack on his back like a donkey. "He had so worn himself down by fasting and vigil that he looked like a death's-head, mere bone and skin."[26] William had given up the realms of earthly nobility to save his own soul by suffering, self-denial, and purgation. This was the medieval religious system, a system of self-effort and suffering to gain the halls of paradise—a system that included relics, purgatory, penance, fear, and uncertainty, without providing assurance that one had ever done enough. Years later that 14-year-old would commit himself to this system in hopes of gaining a clean conscience and assurance that he would one day be in heaven.

The young boy, of course, was Martin Luther. No matter how hard he tried to get to heaven by "monkery" or by plumbing the depths of the mystic's surrender to God, he could never be calm before the majesty, justice, and holiness of God. The more he tried to please God, the more he hated him. Over time, however, as Luther studied the Scriptures, rediscovering the good news of the gospel freed his tormented conscience.

For Luther, there were five critical elements to the true gospel:

1. The distinction between the law and the gospel
2. The doctrine of justification by faith alone
3. The definitions of repentance and faith
4. The bondage and inability of man's will concerning salvation
5. The reality of sin in the Christian's life and the subsequent need to live daily by the gospel

The first four elements explain and buttress one another. The fifth underscores the fact that the believer is at the same time just and sinful. This last point is critical, for if we do not understand this reality, we will doubt the grace of God and plunge ourselves either into arrogance or despair. This chapter will examine these five aspects so that we might gain greater clarity, joy, and assurance in knowing the gospel.[27]

The Distinction between the Law and the Gospel

How much commitment to God is enough for a person to be saved? How much obedience to the commands of God must one give in order to go to heaven? How much sacrifice and how much faith? Luther rightly noted from Scripture that full obedience to the law of God—both in actions and in heart—must be rendered *throughout a person's life* to go to heaven. The law demands a pure, holy, unalloyed obedience given from birth to death, without sin, condemning absolutely anyone who does not obey perfectly. And so, as we observed in chapter one, Luther tried to render this radical obedience to the law. He failed. He then learned that in all history, Christ is the only one who kept the law, the only one who surrendered in perfect obedience.

This leads us to the pure good news of the gospel. The gospel is an announcement about what Christ has done on our behalf. As both God and man, Jesus is the only one in all of history who could actually keep the law perfectly and have that obedience credited to us. Thus, there is no adding of our obedience to the work of Christ: no need for it, and no possibility of it.

Luther considered an understanding of God's law and the gospel (and the distinction between the two) essential to comprehending the entire Bible and coming to truly know God. This distinction taught in the Scriptures brings immeasurable peace and comfort to the believer.

- Without this distinction, one is left with his own efforts in trying to earn heaven by obeying God's

commands, all the while kept from knowing and
embracing the free, joyful, and glorious promise
found in the message of the gospel.

- Without this distinction, the gospel turns into
command, rather than an announcement of good
news of what God has done for the sinner.

- Without this distinction, one is left with a false religion,
in which man ascends to God by his own righteousness, wisdom, and good works (1 Corinthians 1:21).

For Luther, being able to distinguish between the
word of God's law and the word of God's gospel was the
essence of true Christianity:

> Distinguishing between the law and the gospel is the
> highest art in Christendom, one who every person
> who values the name Christian ought to recognize,
> know, and possess. Where this is lacking, it is not
> possible to tell who is a Christian and who is a pagan
> or Jew. That much is at stake in this distinction.[28]

Luther defined "law" as all of God's commands both
in the Old and New Testaments and "gospel" as all of the
promises in Scripture, freely given in and through Christ,
apart from our works—by sheer grace. "We should
understand 'law' to mean nothing else than God's word
and command, in which he directs us what to do and
what not to do, and demands from us our obedience and
'work.'"[29] He then defines the gospel:

> On the other hand, the gospel or the faith is a doctrine
> or word of God that does not require our works. *It*

46

does not command us to do anything. On the contrary, it bids us merely to accept the offered grace of forgiveness of sins and eternal life and let it be given to us. It means that we do nothing; only receive, and allow ourselves to be given what has been granted to us and handed to us in the Word.[30]

Luther hereby reminds us that the law and gospel are two entirely distinct categories: law is not gospel, gospel is not law. The beauty and power of each vanish when they are blended together. The perfection and majesty of the law is compromised, and the announcement of the good news that Christ kept the law for us and suffered the curse of the law for us is entirely lost. Blending the two leads one into suffocating moralism, anguished guilt, or a lofty legalism that destroys everything and everyone in its wake. The pure message of Christ keeping the law for us becomes lost.

In his 1535 *Lectures on Galatians*, Luther explains in greater depth the inability of anyone on earth to be made just in God's sight by obedience to the law or to have a conscience set at peace by good works:

For the law requireth perfect obedience unto God, and condemneth all those that do not accomplish the same. Now, it is certain that there is no man living which is able to perform this obedience; which notwithstanding God straitly requireth of us: the law therefore justifieth not, but condemneth, according to that saying: "Cursed is he that abideth not in all things written in this law," &c. (Deut. xxvii. 26; Gal. iii. 10).[31]

In speaking of the monks' efforts to be justified by keeping the law, he writes,

> Neither is it possible for them to have quietness and peace of conscience in great and inward terrors, and in the agony of death, yea though they have observed the law, loved their neighbours, done many good works, and suffered great afflictions: for the law always terrifieth and accuseth, saying: Thou never didst accomplish all that is commanded in the law; but accursed is he that hath not done all things contained therein, &c. Wherefore these terrors remain still in the conscience and increase more and more.[32]

What then was the primary purpose of the law for Luther? To show us the truth about ourselves before a holy God and drive us to look for righteousness outside of ourselves. All the law can do is show us our guilt and present us naked before God. Referring to Israel's terror at the foot of Sinai as the law was given, Luther wrote,

> So the proper office of the law is to lead us out of our tents and tabernacles, that is to say, from the quietness and security wherein we dwell, and from trusting in ourselves, and to bring us before the presence of God, to reveal his wrath unto us, and to set before us our sins. Here the conscience feeleth that it hath not satisfied the law, neither is it able to satisfy it, nor to bear the wrath of God. [33]

Luther's teaching here is extremely important. He is saying that the law of God is what God uses to bring us before the face of God—"into the sight of God." It is one thing to know the right theological phrases. It is another thing to be brought into the sight of God by the Holy Spirit using the preaching of the law in order that we may see our true condition. It is at this point that our consciences are taught of God and we treasure the gospel of grace with all our hearts. Some in our day are critical of talk about grace, for such talk can devolve into trivializing the holiness of God. Yet to those who have been taught the lesson of the law—to those who have begun to see the holiness of God and their own sin in the light of God's holiness—grace means everything. It is all such a person has.

Luther wrote,

> When a man is thus taught and instructed by the law, then is he terrified and humbled, then he seeth indeed the greatness of his sin, and cannot find in himself one spark of the love of God: therefore he justifieth God in his Word, and confesseth that he is guilty of death and eternal damnation. The first part then of Christianity is the preaching of repentance, and the knowledge of ourselves… Wherefore the law doth nothing else but utter sin, terrify, and humble, and by this means prepareth us to justification, and driveth us to Christ.[34]

In his teaching on the law, Luther was expounding what God has said through the epistle of Romans:

> Now we know that whatever the law says, it speaks to those who are under the law, so that every mouth may be closed and all the world may become accountable to God; because by the works of the law

no flesh will be justified in his sight; for through the
law comes the knowledge of sin (3:19, 20).

In his sermon on Isaiah 9:6, where Christ is called
"Everlasting Father," Luther explains how faith in Christ
frees us from the law's condemnation:

> When you, therefore, believe on Christ, the law has
> no further claim on you. For all eternity Christ does
> not wish to condemn you, but to be your Father, and
> you his child… This we must learn well, that above
> all things Christ in his kingdom does not wish to
> condemn, but to forgive, and to be our everlasting
> Father… If there's need for the law, however, then
> let it be laid against your flesh, to keep it chaste and
> submissive to God's Ten Commandments. Your faith,
> however, your heart and conscience, must remain
> free from the law and by virtue of this name, "Ever-
> lasting Father," should crush the law in your heart,
> like ice melts before the summer's heat.[35]

As Philip Watson explains, the law of God humbles
us and removes all hope in our own righteousness.

> [The law] no longer prescribed the terms and condi-
> tions of salvation, but was the hammer of God to
> break down man's pride and self-reliance and drive
> him to surrender in faith to the forgiveness and grace
> revealed in Christ, and supremely in his cross. By the
> fire of this grace, the entire medieval Catholic scheme
> of salvation, with every thought of merit and worthi-
> ness, was reduced to ashes.[36]

The law causes us to seek a righteousness outside of ourselves, the righteousness found only in the gospel promise and the righteousness that comes only by faith alone. Thus the law/gospel distinction leads us to the critical doctrine of justification by faith alone, which Luther believed was the heart of the gospel.

Justification by Faith Alone

In our contemporary culture we have little idea of the need to be declared righteous before a holy God, for we are dim to the majesty and holiness of God and therefore have a high estimate of ourselves. Yet Luther rightly understood these things. The majesty of God required man's perfect obedience to the law, a perfection man could never render. To Luther, therefore, the issue of justification by faith alone was *the* issue of the day.

Luther saw that a sinner who simply looked to the Lord Jesus by faith alone—by trusting in *Christ's* work and not personal performance or supposed righteousness—was freely pardoned, loved, forgiven, and fully accepted by God. Jesus' perfect obedience to his own law met the righteous requirements of the law for the believer, and his death on the cross once and for all paid the debt for the believer's sin. He realized the life and death of Christ were credited to the believer, securing for him or her a perfect righteousness, *permanently* freed from all wrath. Hence, there was now no condemnation for those in Christ Jesus (Romans 8:1). The believer was fully justified, declared righteous before God.

Luther grasped the fact that sinners were *declared* righteous by God apart from any of their works, whereas the Church in Luther's day taught that sinners were *made* righteous in actual conduct as they cooperated with God's grace. *This actual righteousness, the Church taught, was the means by which a person was justified before God.* Luther understood the subtle yet damning error in this teaching, for while it acknowledged God's grace as *helping* the sinner to obey, it placed salvation back into the efforts of man and removed the objective peace of God that rested entirely in Christ alone.

Luther understood justification by faith alone to be central to the gospel and to Christianity: "For if the article of justification be once lost, then is all true Christian doctrine lost."[37] This justification occurred not by human works, resolve, or cooperation with the Spirit's work within him, but rather by simple faith—trusting the person and work of Christ alone, apart from any self-righteousness or law-keeping. Toward the end of his life, Luther reflected back on the period when the doctrine of justification broke into his life and brought peace to his troubled conscience:

> Then I grasped that the justice of God is that righteousness by which through grace and sheer mercy God justifies us through faith. Thereupon I felt myself to be reborn and to have gone through the open doors into paradise. The whole of Scripture took on a new meaning, and whereas before the "justice of God" had filled me with hate, now it became to me inexpressibly sweet in greater love. This passage of Paul became to me a gate of heaven.[38]

The righteousness of Christ—his perfect obedience to the law and his death for our sins freely imputed (credited) to us by faith alone—is a righteousness *outside of us*, not based on any sanctification that the Holy Spirit accomplishes in us: "But Christ is its perfect and entire holiness; and where [our internal holiness] is not enough, Christ is enough."[39]

Commenting on Galatians 3:6, "Abraham believed God and it was reckoned to him as righteousness," Luther writes concerning imputed righteousness,

> If thou believe, thou art righteous, because thou givest glory unto God, that he is almighty, merciful, true, etc… And the sin which remaineth in thee, is not laid to thy charge, but is pardoned for Christ's sake in whom thou believest, who is perfectly just; whose righteousness is thy righteousness, and thy sin is his sin.[40]

Luther constantly taught the gospel and justification, for man is ever prone to live by works rather than by grace. He also considered the doctrine of justification as being of great pastoral comfort for the believer troubled by his sin: "We therefore do make this definition of a Christian, that a Christian is not he which hath no sin, or feeleth no sin, but he to whom God imputeth not his sin because of his faith in Christ. This doctrine bringeth strong consolation to afflicted consciences in serious and inward terrors."[41]

Forgiveness of sins—apart from works, law, purgatory, or indulgences—was freely given in Christ alone, rendering the believing sinner righteous before a holy God, with all the demands of his law fully met by the Savior. This was the assurance and peace a believer gained through the doctrine of justification by faith alone.

The promise of the gospel—specifically, being

justified by faith alone and not by works—was what Luther considered to be *the* difference between the true and living God and all other gods, which were merely idols. In his lectures on Psalm 51, Luther noted that all other gods besides the true and living God, no matter their name, are simply one and the same god—a god who masquerades as Jehovah, but is in fact merely a god without mercy, knowing only justice and wrath. He is a god without the promise of grace, a god before whom we could never be justified. To encounter God without his offer of grace is to destroy ourselves.

Luther's distinction between god the absolute (the false gods who relate to us by works) and the God of promise was a brilliant observation. All the religions of the world that seek justification through law (no matter what form this law may take) are worshiping a false god. Even those who may belong to a Protestant church but are still seeking to be justified by works are worshiping the "absolute god" (to use Luther's phrase), who is really no god at all but rather an idol. Only in true Christianity can the living and true God—the God of promise—be found. Only before the God of promise can we stand justified by faith alone. Only by the promise of the gospel can we have goodness and mercy follow us all the days of our life and know the sweetness and joy of God's abiding love. In other words, only in Jesus Christ is the promise of grace found, given, and enjoyed.

To the soul convicted of sin, standing before a god without grace is frightening beyond description. There is no hope before such a god, but only great fear and crushing despair. Yet to this same burdened soul the God of promise is sweet beyond all comparison. The promises of the gospel and of justification freely given on account of the work of another become to him better than life, giving him inexpressible hope and joy. He is at peace because he sees that there is no sin too great to be forgiven, for Christ died once for all sin. Luther treasured the God of promise and the truth of his free justification. He gave his life to this promise.

Repentance and Faith

Luther's definition of the words "repentance" and "faith" reveal a third integral aspect of his understanding of the gospel. He stood against the Roman Catholic Church's definition of these words that undercut the free gospel of grace. Incorrect definitions of these terms would ruin the entire gospel message. In our day as well, the gospel is often lost because we have vague definitions of these terms—definitions that insert works and human effort back into the gospel. Therefore it is crucial to be clear on what repentance and faith actually mean.

The Roman practice of penance. The Church in Luther's day had developed a system of penance in which three steps had to be accomplished for the successful penitent to merit forgiveness. First he needed *contrition*, a lamenting all his known sins. Next came verbal *confession*, where he had to list all his known sins to a confessor, humiliating himself with sorrow. The final step was *satisfaction*, where the priest prescribed actions for the penitent to complete in order to pay for his sins. Whatever was missed in this process was to be made up by punishment in purgatory.

Roland Bainton, a twentieth-century church historian, notes that this erroneous system of penance had its roots in Jerome's mistranslation of a Greek word in the Latin

Vulgate. In his translation of Matthew 4:17 ("Repent, for the kingdom of heaven is at hand"), Jerome translated the Greek word as "do penance" rather than "to be penitent." Luther called the correcting of this error a "glowing" discovery.[42] He pointed out the folly of Rome's false system and the uncertain state of forgiveness it yielded. How could a sinner know if he was contrite enough or if he had made sufficient confession? The Smalcald Articles state,

> Each person had to enumerate all of his or her sins (which is impossible). This was a great torment. Whatever the person had forgotten was forgiven only on the condition that when it was remembered it had to be confessed. Under these circumstances people could never know whether they had confessed perfectly enough or whether confession would ever end.[43]

According to the practice of penance, a sufficient work and sacrifice needed to be made in order for the penalty of sin to be satisfied. Of course, such satisfaction was also ambiguous: how much sacrifice was sufficient for full satisfaction? The notion of satisfaction added to the perfect and finished work of Christ on the cross.

Repentance. Against this introspection, Luther understood the biblical word for "repent" to simply mean "a change of mind." Specifically, it meant to change one's mind about the entirety of his life—that he has no righteousness to offer before God. He wrote, "[Repentance] simply lumps everything together and says, 'Everything is pure sin with us. [Why] would we want to spend so much time investigating, dissecting, or distinguishing [individual sins, as is done in penance]?'"[44]

To repent is simply to see that nothing good dwells in our hearts and to therefore look entirely outside of ourselves to the Savior. How can we ever "scrape the bottom of the barrel" of our sinfulness and sinful motives? Any attempt to understand and analyze our sin is never-ending (cf. Jeremiah 17:9 and Psalm 51:3–5). We must admit we are depraved and then take our condition to the cross. This brings assurance and frees us from intro-spective attempts to plumb the depths of our sin and our motives. It also gives all glory to God, for in this definition we cannot offer a single good work toward our salvation, and we see God's abundant and free grace in forgiving.

Faith. Concerning the word *faith*, Luther said it was diametrically opposed to any work. Rather, faith was reliance on the gospel promise, trusting in the person and work of Christ. For Luther, faith was not a vague "faith in God," or a merely generic faith in the Bible, but *a specific trust that holds Jesus as its sole object*.

In his sermon on the Syrophoenician woman (Matthew 15:21–28), Luther described faith as, "a hearty trust in the grace and goodness of God as experienced and revealed through his Word."[45] Faith, for Luther, was a clinging to Christ and the promises of the gospel, a resting in Christ and not in one's own works. He under-stood faith as confidence that God is good and true to his promise of grace to those who believe.

Our reason says we should give works to God. Faith teaches that we cannot give works but must trust Christ alone. Such trust in the goodness of God goes against what we naturally perceive or reason to be true. Our circumstances may seem to affirm that God hates us, but faith clings to the pure, objective Word of God and his promise of grace in spite of what the world, our own heart and reason, or the devil might say.

The Roman Catholic view of faith in the sixteenth century defined it as trust *and* obedience (works). The Church stated that faith could not be raw trust that stood alone apart from works, but rather that faith had to produce works, and that these works *themselves* would justify man before God. This "justifying faith," as Rome termed it, was faith forming itself by love — that is, love for God and love for one's neighbor.

This view ultimately turned faith into obedience to the law, rather than simple trust in Christ alone. Luther rejected this concept of justifying faith. He believed it would cause man to seek justification by works of the law once again, looking to be justified not through trust alone, but by his love for God and neighbor. In his commentary on Galatians 2:16, Luther warned against the teaching that faith only justified someone when love and good works are added to it.

Two terms taught by the Church of Luther's day — *congruity* and *condignity* — help to further explain Rome's view of faith that Luther encountered. Though we may be unfamiliar with these terms today, the errors of congruity and condignity have their subtle echo in some present-day Protestant thinking, eroding the truth of faith in Christ.

If a person was outside a state of grace and in what the Church called *mortal sin* (a category of sin that utterly damns a person and is unforgivable),[46] he could do a work of *congruity* (for example, give alms or hear the Mass) whereby he would receive spiritual strength to do good works of *condignity*. These works of *condignity* were actual good works done with God's help that earned eternal life.

Such teaching made trust in Christ and his death on the cross unnecessary. It emerged from a high view of man's ability and a shallow view of sin and depravity (and thus a low view of God's holiness).

By contrast, Luther realized that one's best works—even works done by grace—are full of deeply rooted sin and impurity. He saw that when a man became convinced of the depth of his sin and depravity, he would conclude that he has absolutely no good works to offer a holy God. Even with the Holy Spirit's help in producing works within a person, man could still not be justified by these works, for even these works were tainted with sin.

In addition to combating the concepts of condignity and congruity, Luther's definition of faith and his belief in the sufficiency of faith alone confronted one other aspect of Catholicism: the teaching that the Mass had the power to grant forgiveness. "The sacraments, especially the Mass, were the central piece in the piety of the late medieval church. Through them the church transmitted the grace of God to sinners and turned their partial confessions, partial good works, and partial faith into deeds that were truly pleasing to God."[47] Against all this, Luther taught a simple trust in Jesus Christ alone—without any work whatsoever from man. In other words, faith does not involve any reliance upon ourselves at all. Rather, it is a raw, bare, and simple trust in the promises of God as found in the gospel message.

This biblical understanding of repentance and faith that Luther treasured and taught was key to his understanding of the gospel. He found inexpressible joy in the gospel as a result. As quoted earlier, "If you have a true faith that Christ is your Saviour, then at once you have a gracious God, for

faith leads you in and opens up God's heart and will, that
you should see pure grace and overflowing love."[48]

Such biblical faith and repentance meant that man
was unable to offer God any personal righteousness or
to add any merit to the work of Christ. Man, in fact, was
so dead in sins that even faith and repentance had to be
given to man as an undeserved, gracious gift from God.
Man was unable to believe, bound in his will, requiring
the work of a gracious Savior. These facts, which we will
discuss more in the following section, were the foundation of Luther's understanding of the gospel.

Man's Inability and the Bondage of the Will

It was September of 1524 when the great Humanist
scholar, Desiderius Erasmus, published *Diatribe*, which
we mentioned briefly in chapter one. This was Erasmus'
first public attack on Luther's teaching. In it, he opposed
Luther's view of free will. Erasmus believed that Christian
conduct—good morals and right behavior—was the
primary way by which people could please God, and he
downplayed Luther's emphasis on salvation being a matter
of God's grace, not man's works. J.I. Packer and O.R.
Johnston have observed that Erasmus did not even consider
free will to be an especially significant issue. Instead,
Erasmus believed that Luther had blown the doctrine's
importance out of proportion.[49] In other words, Erasmus
accused Luther of making much ado about nothing.

Erasmus' approach seemed humble and self-depre-
cating, which is often how false teaching comes across
as reasonable and acceptable to the general public. But
Luther found Erasmus' attack and his trivialization of free

will infuriating. In response, Luther cast off all restraint: he responded by writing his blistering work, *On the Bondage of the Will,* which attacked the teaching that man's will is free with respect to salvation.

Three Problems with Free Will

Salvation by works. Luther understood free will as being at the very heart of the gospel. He realized that if man's will is truly free, then man is capable of keeping God's law perfectly and thus earning a right standing with God.

Remember that Luther had tried himself to behave perfectly before God, and failed. Every monk he had ever known had failed. Every Jew in the Old Testament—indeed, every person in the Bible, except Jesus, had failed. To Luther, Scripture itself explained why free will was a false notion, and therefore why every person other than Jesus has always failed and will always fail to behave in a way that God finds acceptable.

In other words, Luther realized that if man's will is free, *he can save himself through works,* without any help from the perfect life and sacrificial death of Christ on the cross.

Salvation by decision. Luther also recognized a second, separate, fundamental problem: if man has free will *he can choose to believe.* This means that a person with free will can—indeed, he must—contribute to his own salvation. Such a choice thus becomes a necessary element of every Christian's salvation. A person's eternal destiny thus comes to rest in his or her own decision, rather than in the sovereign decree of the Triune God.

Shared glory. Finally, Luther noted that if one held to the doctrine of free will, glory does not go to God alone. It is shared with man who has *chosen* God.

For all these reasons, Luther thought the concept of free will established man as judge and arbiter over God. He keenly observed that Erasmus's thoughts started with man and not with God. Therefore, in writing to Erasmus he stated, "Your thoughts of God are too human."[50]

Two Fruits of Rejecting Free Will

If man does not have free will with respect to salvation, then we must consider his will in this area to be bound. In *On the Bondage of the Will,* Luther gave two reasons why the doctrine of man's bound will is critical to understanding the nature of the gospel.

Humility. When man comes to see his will as bound, his pride is humbled and he begins to understand grace:

> God has surely promised his grace to the humbled: that is, to those who mourn over and despair of themselves. But a man cannot be thoroughly humbled till he realises that his salvation is utterly beyond his own powers, counsels, efforts, will, and works, and depends absolutely on the will, counsel, pleasure, and work of another—God alone.[51]

Faith. The teaching that man's will is bound safeguards the nature of faith: man must walk by faith and not by sight, by what God has declared rather than by what he thinks should be true. "Faith's object is things unseen. That there may be room for faith, therefore, all that is believed must be hidden... Thus, when God quickens, He does so by killing; when He justifies, He does so by pronouncing guilty; when He carries up to heaven, He does so by bringing down to hell."[52] The scriptural teaching of man's will being bound forces one either to humbly trust God's wisdom or to rely on man's own reasoning.

"Am I of the Elect?"

Luther knew that the teaching of the bondage of the will, along with predestination (that before the creation of the universe God had already selected specific individuals to be saved) should be handled pastorally. For those who wondered if they were of the elect (that is, predestined), he warned against trying to answer this question *by looking at predestination*; if one did this, he would be driven to endless despair and caught in a firestorm of anguish and doubt. Rather, *look at Christ and the gospel promise*. Hear the good news and believe!

It's actually not complicated: *if you want Christ and the gospel, you are one of his elect*. This is how you will know if you are God's child. To start instead with predestination would be to try to climb into heaven and see the hidden counsel of God, which will crush a person. One should not build his or her assurance on the hidden counsel of God—that is, by starting with the question, "Am I elect?" Rather, Luther counseled to begin with Christ and his being freely offered and known by the promise of the gospel offer. It would be disastrous and absurd to build one's faith and assurance on the secret counsel of God's predestination. Rather, build on the foundation: Christ. Here, the Lord is freely offered and freely known. Only by starting with Christ the foundation can one move on to knowing that one is predestined.

Luther's younger contemporary, John Calvin, was of one heart with Luther regarding this counsel. Calvin went to great length in his *Institutes* in pastorally handling predes-

tination and urged one to look *only* at Christ to know if one
was saved. The only safe way one could consider his own
election was by looking at Jesus and the free gospel offer.

He who believes has everlasting life. Don't look at
anything from within you. Don't try to discover the hidden
counsel of God. Rather, simply believe the good news of
great joy. The promise of the gospel is the primary way,
Calvin taught, that one can be assured that he or she is elect.

The bondage of the will was a treasured theme for
Luther that went back to his early years as a reformer — to
1518, when he wrote his Heidelberg Disputation. He
considered the truth of man's bound will to be a doctrine
that gave all glory to God and humbled man's pride; it
safeguarded grace (Theses 13–18 of the Disputation)
and let God be God. Indeed, this theme was precious
to Luther and appeared in his teaching to the end of his
days. (Luther's Heidelberg Disputation will be more fully
discussed in chapter three).

At the Same Time Just and Sinful

Those who have read anything of Luther's life and
theology will be familiar with his phrase, *simul iustus et
peccator.*[53] That is, the true Christian who has trusted
Christ alone for salvation is *at the same time* just before
God and also a sinner. Perhaps the chief passage for this
truth is found in Romans 7:14–20, where Paul confesses his
failure to obey the law of God and to avoid that which he
should not do. Yet Paul did not lose his justification before
God, for he stood before the majesty of God not by his
own record of obedience but by the obedience of Christ.

Luther grasped this reality and believed that a

wholehearted embracing of this truth was critical to appropriating the gospel and living in the joy and freedom of the gospel.

> For as long as I live in the flesh, sin is truly in me. But because I am covered under the shadow of Christ's wings, as is the chicken under the wing of the hen, and dwell without all fear under that most ample and large heaven of the forgiveness of sins… And although we see [our sin], and for the same do feel the terrors of conscience, yet flying unto Christ our mediator and reconciler (through whom we are made perfect), we are sure and safe… Thus a Christian man is both righteous and a sinner, holy and profane, an enemy of God and yet a child of God. [54]

Christian culture today is saturated with messages from well-meaning Bible teachers who long to see believers living "the victorious Christian life." Although such perfectionistic, higher-life teaching comes in many forms, at the core is the message that if one follows a particular program of surrender (or repentance or other works-based techniques), he or she will rise above known sin. Though few actually claim that a Christian can be perfect, these method-based teachings do imply that such attainment can be ours if we work long and hard enough.

This general message can be traced to a compromise on the doctrine of man. In the late 1700s and early 1800s, much of the Western church came to embrace various forms of Pelagianism. Named after a 5th-century teacher, Pelagianism in its original form claimed that man's nature is fundamentally good, and therefore perfect obedience to

God is within man's ability. In Semi-Pelagianism, man is seen as sinful yet still *able* to keep the law of God without sin.

All such Pelagian-influenced views prevent an individual from facing the full reality and implications of sin in his or her life. This often leads either to doubt or arrogance. If I wonder, "How can I be a Christian and still be stuck in this same sinful habit?" I will begin to doubt my salvation, the Bible, or both. If I think I am actually keeping the law of God and meeting his standard of perfection, I will become arrogant. Any sort of perfectionistic belief will also tempt me to judge and condemn others for their failings and indwelling sin. I will respond in pride to Christian brothers and sisters, rather than in humility and gentleness.

Perfectionism may have had a slightly different form in Luther's day, but he still encountered this false theology. Naturally, he faced it squarely and rejected it, considering it to be a denial of the gospel. His biblical observation of *simul iustus et peccator* allowed the believer to face the truth of his life, while still enjoying confident acceptance by God in the gospel.

The truth that the believer is at the same time justified before God and yet still a sinner is a doctrine we must know, lest we be driven to despair and discouragement. Others have also believed and taught this doctrine. For example, The Heidelberg Catechism, written 17 years after Luther's death, answers a significant question after looking at the law of God: "But can those who are converted to God perfectly keep these commandments? No, but even the holiest of men, while in this life, have only a small beginning of this obedience." (HC 114)

Making a similar point nearly 130 years later, the Puritan Thomas Watson wrote,

> Man is a self-exalting creature; and if he has anything but of worth, he is ready to be puffed up; but when he comes to see his deficiencies and failings, and how far short he comes of the holiness and perfection which God's law requires, it pulls down the plumes of his pride, and lays them in the dust; he weeps over his inability; he blushes over his leprous spots… God lets this inability [to keep his law] upon us, that we may have recourse to Christ to obtain pardon for our defects, and to sprinkle our best duties with his blood. When a man sees that he owes perfect obedience to the law, but has nothing to pay, it makes him flee to Christ to be his friend, and answer for him all the demands of the law, and set him free in the court of justice.[55]

The great Princeton professor A.A. Hodge was also quick to see the reality of sin in the believer's life:

> The more holy a man is, the more humble, self-renouncing, self-abhorring, and the more sensitive to every sin he becomes, and the more closely he clings to Christ. The moral imperfections which cling to him he feels to be sins, laments and strives to overcome them… it has been notoriously the fact that the best Christians have been those who have been the least prone to claim the attainment of perfection for themselves.[56]

Another Princeton professor, Benjamin Breckenridge Warfield, wrote hundreds of pages confronting the errors

of perfectionism and the idea that saints no longer are
sinners. In his essay on "Miserable-Sinner Christianity,"
Warfield did a masterful job of showing how throughout
Protestant history and across all denominations and confessions, the Protestant church has always held to Luther's
doctrine that the believer is at the same time sinful and
justified. In his day, such a belief was mockingly labeled,
"miserable-sinner Christianity." In his essay, Warfield
observed that such Christianity was the only true Christianity! Yet such Christianity was far from being morose,
despairing, and joyless. Rather, it was the only kind of
Christianity that knew true and unbounding joy and
freedom from despair. "Miserable-sinner Christianity"
was the only kind of Christianity that faced the reality
of sin in the Christian life and at the same time knew the
unchanging love of God for his children. Such Christianity also produced genuine humility, as Warfield explained:

> It belongs to the very essence of the type of Christian-
> ity propagated by the Reformation that the believer
> should feel himself continuously unworthy of the
> grace by which he lives… We must always be accepted
> for Christ's sake, or we cannot ever be accepted at
> all. This is not true of us only "when we believe." It is
> just as true after we have believed. It will continue to
> be true as long as we live. Our need of Christ does not
> cease with our believing; nor does the nature of our
> relation to him or to God through him ever alter, no
> matter what our attainments in Christian graces or our
> achievements in Christian behavior may be. It is always
> on his "blood and righteousness" alone that we rest.[57]

In referring to the joy that "miserable-sinner Christianity" produces, Warfield noted:

> The spirit of this Christianity is a spirit of penitent indeed, but overmastering exultation. The attitude of the "miserable sinner" is not only not one of despair; it is not even one of depression; and not even one of hesitation or doubt; hope is too weak of a word to apply to it. It is an attitude of exultant joy. Only this joy has its ground not in ourselves but in our Savior.[58]

In our own time, noted author Jerry Bridges has often written of the believer's constant need to remember the gospel. We are often accused by the devil and wonder if we are God's child or if God will still love and accept us when we have sinned so deeply. Bridges notes, "The truly godly person never forgets that he was at one time an object of God's holy and just wrath. He never forgets that Christ Jesus came into the world to save sinners, and he feels, along with Paul, that he is himself the worst of sinners."[59] Bridges continues:

> If God's love for us is to be a solid foundation stone of devotion, we must realize that his love is entirely of grace, that it rests completely upon the work of Jesus Christ and flows to us through our union with him. Because of this basis his love can never change, regardless of what we do. In our daily experience, we have all sorts of spiritual ups and downs—sin, failure, discouragement, all of which tend to make us question God's love. That is because we keep thinking that God's love is somehow conditional. We

are afraid to believe his love is based entirely upon the finished work of Christ for us.[60]

These quotes addressing the myth of perfectionism and the reality of indwelling sin in the believer's life help us see that Luther's *simul iustus et peccator* has been understood and believed across the centuries in many denominations. It is not just a Lutheran idea, but one that many different denominations have seen arise from the Scriptures themselves.

The faith of medieval and Renaissance times was a religion of fear and uncertainty, but Luther's understanding of the gospel crashed into this world with joy and assurance. The truth of justification by faith alone, buttressed by the law/gospel distinction, a recovery of correct definitions of repentance and faith, the admission of man's bound will, and the humble acknowledgment of sin in the believer's life brought immeasurable joy and confidence to Luther's tormented conscience and freed him to genuinely love and worship God for the first time.

While there are many branches of the Protestant faith today, all Protestantism has at its beginning Luther's doctrine of justification by faith alone and its centrality to the entire Christian life and the Church. The Dutch theologian Herman Bavinck noted, "there is no essential difference on the doctrine of justification between the Lutheran and the Reformed theology."[61] Elsewhere, Bavinck summarized Luther's impact: "He again grasped the gospel as a glorious message of grace and forgiveness and brought religion back into religion. As a result he has proven fruitful for the whole theological and dogmatic enterprise."[62]

- In his often-quoted statement, Calvin considered justification to be "the principle hinge on which religion is supported."
- Patrick Hamilton, trained by Luther's collaborator Melanchthon and the early Lutherans, took the gospel to Scotland, outlining a law/gospel distinction.
- John Knox (who began Presbyterianism in Scotland) treasured Hamilton's theology and witness.
- Later Presbyterians, such as J. Gresham Machen in the U.S., would preach the gospel with clarity and simplicity.
- Other men such as the Dutch theologian Herman Witsius would continue to proclaim a free gospel, giving clear distinction between works and grace.
- Two of the founders of Methodism, John and Charles Wesley, both came to trust Christ alone for salvation as they heard Luther's commentaries read.[63]
- Anglicans such as Richard Hooker and Augustus Toplady in England also clearly taught the gospel (see also *Anglicanism's 39 Articles of Religion*, written by Thomas Cranmer).
- Baptists such as Charles Spurgeon and Edward Mote (who wrote the hymn, "The Solid Rock"), would also come to preach the gospel with one voice with Luther.

Indeed, another entire book could be written on how the Protestant faith in its varied branches have treasured the gospel as Luther taught it.

On the other hand, while we may not bow to the bones of saints or fear purgatory, in many places Protestantism in our day has fallen into the same ambiguity and confusion about the gospel that existed in medieval Christianity. We have blurred the distinction between the law and the gospel and have lost the doctrine of justification. We have forgotten Christ *for* us and have sought peace in Christ's subjective work *in* us. We have gloried in our own decision to become a Christian. In the air that we breathe are subtle forms of perfectionism that will not allow us to admit our sin and ongoing need for forgiveness and the finished work of Christ; we have forgotten the truth of *simul iustus et peccator.* Returning to the biblical gospel that Luther recovered is *the* critical need of our day. Such a return will cause us to give glory to God.

> With thee is naught but untold grace
> Evermore forgiving.
> We cannot stand before thy face,
> Not by the best of living.
> No man boasting may draw near.
> All the living stand in fear.
> Thy grace alone can save them.
>
> Therefore in God I place my trust,
> My own claim denying.
> Believe in him alone I must,
> On his sole grace relying.
> He pledged to me his plighted word.
> My comfort is in what I heard.
> There will I hold forever.[64]

Three

THAT NO FLESH SHOULD GLORY IN GOD'S PRESENCE

Two Outworkings of the True Gospel

But God hath chosen the foolish things of the world to
confound the wise;
and God hath chosen the weak things of the world
to confound the things which are mighty;
And base things of the world, and things which are
despised, hath God chosen, yea, and things which are not,
to bring to naught things that are;
That no flesh should glory in his presence.

1 Corinthians 1:27–29 (KJV)

Around A.D. 50 the apostle Paul completed his missionary visit to Athens. He then looked to the western horizon and began his journey to Corinth, a city of power and pride. He had confidently determined to arrive in Corinth with only one weapon in his arsenal: the word of the cross, the message of Jesus Christ and him crucified (1 Corinthians 2:2). A short time after leaving the Corinthian church, under the inspiration of the Holy Spirit Paul wrote to the factious and proud believers of Corinth, rebuking them and reminding them that the gospel leaves no room for arrogance and is diametrically opposed to the so-called "wisdom of the world." The gospel message, its application by God's sovereign decree, and the peculiar choice of those whom God would call by it, left no room for pride. Indeed, the gospel permitted "that no flesh should glory in his presence" (1 Corinthians 1:29).

Just as Paul faced a city of pride with the "foolish" and "weak" message of the cross, so did Martin Luther face a wall of pride in the Holy Roman Empire and her ally, the Roman Catholic Church. It was a world of religious arrogance and self-effort. Luther came to discover the true gospel from the Word of God and, like Paul, was convinced that the gospel gave all glory to God, leaving man humbled. God humbles and strikes the whole world not so much by cataclysmic events, but rather by a weak and foolish message! As Luther noted from the pulpit, "The gospel which [Jesus] placed into the mouths of the apostles is the sword by which he smites the world like thunder and lightning."[65]

Luther loved the message of the cross. Many of his writings highlight the gospel's ability to expose man's depravity, humble his pride, and free him to produce genuine fruit for the glory of God. In chapter one, we observed Luther's personal encounter with the gospel. Chapter two gave attention to what he recognized to be the gospel message. In this chapter, we will see how the gospel message gives all glory to God. We will also see something of the ruckus that occurred as Luther took the gospel in his hands to battle the world. While also drawing from other sources, this chapter will focus briefly on four of Luther's works: *The Heidelberg Disputation* (1518), *The Freedom of the Christian* (1520), *Lectures on Galatians 1–4* (1535), and *Against the Antinomians* (1539).

The Gospel Exposes Man's Inability and Humbles His Pride

In sixteenth century Europe, as we saw in chapter one, the splendor, pomp, and pride of the Renaissance had sunk its roots deep into the Roman Church. Medieval Christianity's mysticism, zeal, and perfectionistic teaching merged with the Renaissance's pride of human achievement. The result was a secular vision of man as a creature of great power, freedom, wisdom, goodness, and nobility. This produced an atmosphere of religious fervor filled with sacrifice, self-purgation, and man-made systems of merit aimed at gaining access to heaven.

Luther did not miss the tragedy of such thinking, and dedicated himself to exposing it for what it truly was—a sham and an illusion. As we mentioned previously, early in his career (1518) Luther presented his *Heidelberg Disputation* to a group of Augustinian monks in Heidelberg, Germany. In it he outlined two categories of thinking he had observed in the Scriptures: the theology of glory and the theology of the cross. It could be argued that it was here, in beginning form, that all the rest of Luther's theology would be found.

Church historian W. Robert Godfrey summarizes Luther's teaching found in *The Heidelberg Disputation:*

He came to talk about the Roman Church's theology of glory: the glory of the use of the human mind and reason to understand theology, the glory of the human experience in gaining merit before God to attain salvation. This theology of glory he contrasted with the theology of the cross where a man comes to recognize that his own mind could not bring him to the truth and his own works could not bring him to God. Only on the cross, the ultimate place of foolishness, was God to be found… Where ought God to be? He ought to be found in the beauty of nature, in the glories of this world. But God was not to be found there. Rather, he was to be found on the cross.[66]

Theses 16–21 of the Disputation explain the core of Luther's argument:

16. The person who believes that he can obtain grace by doing what is in him, adds sin to sin so that he becomes doubly guilty. 17. Nor does speaking in this manner give cause for despair, but for arousing the desire to humble oneself and seek the grace of Christ. 18. It is certain that man must utterly despair of his own ability before he is prepared to receive the grace of Christ. 19. That person does not deserve to be called a theologian who looks upon the invisible things of God as though they were clearly perceptible in those things which [have been created]. 20. That person deserves to be called a theologian, however, who comprehends the visible and manifest things of God through suffering and the cross. 21. A theology

of glory calls evil good and good evil. A theology of the cross calls the thing what it actually is.[67]

In Theses 25 and 26, the beginning of Luther's understanding of justification by faith alone makes its appearance, confronting efforts to be justified before God by keeping the law: "25. He is not righteous who does much, but he who, without work, believes much in Christ. 26. The law says 'do this', and it is never done. Grace says, 'believe in this' and everything is already done."

Elsewhere, Luther wrote concerning the arrogance of the one who trusted his own righteousness:

> To trust in works… is equivalent to giving oneself the honor and taking it from God, to whom fear is due in connection with every work. But this is completely wrong, namely to please oneself in one's own works, and to adore oneself as an idol. He who is self-confident and without the fear of God, however, acts entirely in this manner. For if he had fear he would not be self-confident, and for this reason he would not be pleased with himself, but he would be pleased with God.[68]

The following chart compares the theology of glory and the theology of the cross:[69]

The Theology of Glory	The Theology of the Cross
God gives added grace to those who cooperate with his initial gift of energizing grace.	God gives unmerited favor (grace) to those who are dead, unable to do anything.
God is known only by what is seen and knowledge of God is limited to the reason of man alone. (Man's reason is judge over God's revelation).	God's invisible attributes are seen only through suffering, weakness, and the cross.
Calls evil good and good evil.	Sees things as they actually are—as God sees them— by believing what the Scriptures say, rather than one's own reason.

The Theology of Glory	The Theology of the Cross
Man can earn favor with God by keeping the law of God.	The law crushes and kills and shows man's inability to save himself.
Man *becomes* righteous before God by his own works (even works done with God's help). Man climbs to God by such works.	Man is *declared* righteous before God (justified) by faith alone. God descends down to man apart from man's works.
God loves the lovely and rejects the unlovely.	God loves the unlovable and makes them pleasing in his sight.

In Theses 13–15, Luther attacks belief in free will as it applies to salvation. This laid the foundation for his later book, *On the Bondage of the Will* (discussed in chapter 2), which showed that man, left to himself, cannot and will not choose God or do one good work:

13. Free will, after the fall, exists in name only, and as long as it does what it is able to do, it commits a mortal sin. 14. Free will, after the fall, has power to do good only in a passive capacity, but it can do evil in an evil capacity. 15. Nor could the free will remain in a state of innocence, much less do good, in an active capacity, but only in a passive capacity.

Though the world did not give much immediate notice to Martin Luther's *Heidelberg Disputation*, the work eventually came to be seen as a key summation of his theology. And it clearly showed how God's wisdom—specifically Jesus Christ and him crucified—laid low the pride of man and exposed his inability. In his *Lectures on Galatians* (1535), Luther continued to teach how the gospel, and specifically justification by faith alone, revealed man's inability and sinfulness, how it humbled his pride and gave all glory to God:

> For we teach that all men are ungodly by nature, and the children of wrath (Eph. ii. 3). We condemn man's free-will, his strength, wisdom, and righteousness, and all religion of man's own devising: and to be short, we say that there is nothing in us that is able to deserve grace and the forgiveness of sins; but we preach that we obtain this grace by the free mercy of God only, for Christ's sake.[70]

He observed that man is always seeking to justify himself and therefore needs the law to crush his pride. Luther discussed how the crushing power of God's law humbles man and leads him to trust Christ alone for salvation, thus giving all glory to God's work, and no glory to the work of man.

> Wherefore the law doth nothing else but utter sin, terrify, and humble, and by this means prepareth us to justification, and driveth us to Christ… For God giveth his gifts freely unto all men, and that is the praise and glory of his divinity. But [those who seek to earn their salvation] will not receive grace and everlasting life of him freely, but will deserve the same by their own works. For this cause they would utterly take from the glory of his divinity. To the end therefore that he may maintain and defend the same, he is constrained to send his law before, which as a lightning and thundering from heaven, may bruise and break those hard rocks. [71]

Elsewhere in *Galatians,* Luther revels in the gospel of grace and says of man's inability, "I attribute everything solely to God and nothing at all to men." He would later recall Staupitz's comments on those truths,

> This doctrine which thou preachest, yieldeth glory and all things else unto God alone, and nothing unto men: for unto God (it is clear as day) there cannot be attributed too much glory, goodness, &c. This saying did then greatly comfort and confirm me. And true it is, that the doctrine of the gospel taketh from men all glory, wisdom, righteousness, &c., and giveth the same to the Creator alone, who maketh all things of nothing.[72]

Luther's teachings on the message of the cross in the *Heidelberg Disputation* and his *Lectures on Galatians* revealed the ability of the cross to give all glory to the triune God and yield no glory to man. The "foolishness" and "weakness" of the gospel message was, in truth, the power of God to humble the pride and arrogance of man who would rather climb to God by good works: "For since in the wisdom of God the world through its wisdom did not come to know God, God was well-pleased through the foolishness of the message preached to save those who believe" (1 Corinthians 1:21).

The Gospel Frees a Person to Produce Fruit for the Glory of God

Luther's critics, however, raised a severe cry of protest, maintaining that his emphasis on the freeness of the gospel and man's inability to be justified by the law indicated that he was not interested in ethics or the Ten Commandments. *If the gospel is free and if one is justified by faith alone apart from the works of the law*, they claimed, *it will lead to lawless living and a loss of desire for obedience in the Christian life.* In short, they argued that such doctrine would not produce godly fruit.

Christians have struggled with the freeness of grace since the days of Paul (see Romans 6:1). This struggle simply demonstrates that we find it extremely difficult in practice to let grace truly be grace, with salvation based completely on the work of Christ alone: *Christ for us* in history, keeping the law for us, dying on a cross for our sins on a Friday afternoon, and rising from the dead for our justification. Luther's critics, slow to embrace these truths and the all-sufficiency of the gospel, were skeptical that any good could come from Luther's teachings.

Against this protest Luther answered that *only* the gospel, truly and freely believed, would produce genuine fruit of the Spirit. After all, who else but the Spirit of God himself could produce the Spirit's fruit? Thus, Luther considered the gospel of grace to be the only doctrine, ultimately, that gives true health, worship, and godliness to the Church. He wrote,

> Wherefore it is very necessary, that this doctrine be kept in continual practice and public exercise both of reading and hearing… Wherefore this doctrine be lost, then is also the whole knowledge of truth, life, and salvation lost and gone. If this doctrine flourish, then all good things flourish, religion, the true service of God, the glory of God, the right knowledge of all things and states of life.[73]

Luther expressed profound concern about the need for Christians to live for the glory of God and produce fruit that magnified Christ. This fruit came directly from faith alone in Christ and was accompanied by true joy that only a believer could possess:

> When we have thus taught faith in Christ, then do we teach also good works. Because thou hast laid hold upon Christ by faith, through whom thou art made righteous, begin now to work well. Love God and thy neighbour, call upon God, give thanks unto him, praise him, confess him. Do good to thy neighbour and serve him: fulfil thine office. These are good

works indeed, which flow out of this faith and this cheerfulness conceived in the heart, for that we have remission of sins freely by Christ.[74]

In 1520 Martin Luther wrote one of his best-known works, *The Freedom of the Christian*. This small book summarized how faith alone in Christ—specifically, justification by faith alone—freed the believer to live for the glory of God and the service of others. "A Christian," Luther said, "is a perfectly free lord of all, subject to none. A Christian is a perfectly dutiful servant of all, subject to all."[75]

The Christian is a lord, united to Christ the King, utterly free from the demand of the law as a basis of being saved. Yet, he now gladly serves God and his neighbor, having been set free from sin, death's sting, and the condemnation of the law. The rest of *The Freedom of the Christian* expounds this fact, demonstrating that the fruit of the Spirit comes from the person who has faith alone in Christ. The soul that clings to God's promises, and is therefore glad, will joyfully live in obedience: "Is not such a soul most obedient to God in all things by this faith?… This obedience, however, is not rendered by works, but by faith alone."[76]

What man is there whose heart, upon hearing these things, will not rejoice to its depth, and when receiving such comfort will not grow tender so that he will love Christ as he never could by means of any laws or works?[77]

The inner man, who by faith is created in the image of God, is both joyful and happy because of Christ in whom so many benefits are conferred upon him; and therefore it is his one occupation to serve God joyfully and without thought of gain, in love that is not constrained.[78]

In an often-quoted passage from *The Freedom of the Christian*, Luther points out that an individual can only produce good fruit if he is first made a good person by God. This being made a good person is the product of justification by faith alone. A self-righteous person who continues to trust his own works is still a "bad tree," incapable of producing good fruit:

> Good works do not make a good man, but a good man does good works; evil works do not make a wicked man, but a wicked man does evil works. Consequently it is always necessary that the substance or person himself be good before there can be any good works, and that good works follow and proceed from the good person.[79]

Particularly troublesome to Luther in this area were the Antinomians, a group whose label (meaning "against the law") Luther himself coined and defined. The Antinomians shared Luther's opposition to Rome's view of salvation, yet they fundamentally misunderstood essential elements of Luther's teaching and exaggerated others.

The Antinomians were, at least in theory, the lawless ones that some of Luther's critics had warned of. They actually claimed—not as a criticism of Luther but as a theological position—that since the believer lived now under grace, he no longer needed the Ten Commandments and that therefore little attention was due the Commandments. They also advocated preaching grace first and God's wrath later, claiming this order of preaching as being the best means of bringing people to believe. In his treatise *Against the Antinomians*, written in 1539, Luther sharply rebuked both these errors, expanding on the use of the law in the Christian life, and thus offering us a greater glimpse into his heart toward God's law.

Antinomianism and preaching. *Against the Antinomians* came hard against that group's practice of preaching grace before law. Luther noted that only through the preaching of the law could one be humbled and thus compelled to seek refuge in Christ. If there were no law, there would be no sin. If there were no sin, then there would be no need for a Savior.[80] He pointedly asked, "How can one know what sin is without the law and conscience? And how will we learn what Christ is, what he did for us, if we do not know what the law is that he fulfilled for us and what sin is, for which he made satisfaction?"[81]

Luther also noted that Paul preached in exactly the opposite order from what the Antinomians taught. Paul began with the law so that the gospel and the work of Christ would be clearly seen and embraced. Through the crushing power of the law, people would come to believe the gospel. Thus the law was essential to the life of the Church as well as the life of the individual Christian.[82]

Antinomianism and personal holiness. For Luther, while God gave his commandments primarily for pedagogical use in the Church, they were also to be ethically valued and obeyed. In responding to the Antinomians, he wrote,

> [The Ten Commandments] are daily preached *and practiced* in our churches… Furthermore, the commandments are sung in two versions, as well

as painted, printed, carved, and recited by children morning, noon, and night. *I know of no manner in which we do not use them, unless it be that we unfortunately do not practice and paint them with our deeds and our life as we should.*[83]

Luther clearly loved the Ten Commandments and expected them to be daily held before the believer as well as the unbeliever, and that a fruitful life of obedience to the commandments was to be rendered to God that he might be glorified on earth. In his *Large Catechism* Luther gave careful exposition of each command and clearly expected that the Christian would obey the commands. Yet also in the *Large Catechism* he accurately said that all Christians failed to keep the law, for it was too lofty and majestic for sinful man. The Christian's obedience fell far short of the commands, and therefore one stood before God only by the merits of Christ alone.

In the final analysis, Luther taught that justification by faith alone is the *only* way a person can bear genuine fruit for the glory of God. Yet he also noted the reality of imperfect fruit in even the best Christian life: "As long as we live in the flesh we only begin to make some progress in that which shall be perfected in the future life."[84] The Christian can never put his trust in his works, even works produced by the Holy Spirit, for these works are horribly flawed and inconsistent in light of the perfection of God's law. This side of heaven the Christian's walk and witness will be inconsistent. Therefore we must always relate to God by grace and not by our works. At the same time, the gospel does indeed begin to yield fruit in the believer's life. This is fruit that comes from a joyful, glad, and sincere heart that has been set free by grace and the sure word of God's forgiveness in Christ.

+++

The message of the cross that Paul carried with him to Corinth was the power of God to confront the pride of man (1 Corinthians 1:18–31). This message was, so to speak, the great scythe in the hands of the Lord of glory, laying flat all creation, at once humbling the proud and then comforting the humbled, freeing them to give praise to God. Martin Luther understood this fact and gladly wielded the same message against the social, political, and religious powers of his entire world. He was zealous for the glory of God.

As in the time of medieval and Renaissance Christianity, we live in a day when, even in church, people and ministers regularly attribute glory to man. Few think of giving glory to God. Yet the message of the gospel, rightly understood and believed, frees us to let God be God, that we might forget ourselves and live for his glory. By realizing that our salvation is entirely from God and based completely on Christ's person and work, and by having our hearts set free to love and worship him, we are enabled, without our even realizing it, to produce fruit that truly magnifies Christ—fruit that springs forth from a clean conscience. May the Church heed, once again, the teaching and correction of Luther, so that God and God alone may be glorified among his people.

Four
CHRIST'S CHURCH

Why We Still Need Luther

> *I believe in… the forgiveness of sins.*
> *From the Apostles Creed*

Einar Billing beautifully summarized Luther's thought and theology by the following:

> Anyone who is but a little familiar with Luther knows that his different thoughts are not strung together like pearls in a necklace, united only by the bond of a common authority or perhaps by a chain of logical argument, but that they all lie close as the petals of a rose about a common centre, they shine out like the rays of the sun from one glowing source: the forgiveness of sins. We should be in no danger of misleading the would-be student of Luther, if we expressly gave him the rule: Never imagine you have rightly grasped a Lutheran idea until you have succeeded in reducing it to a simple corollary of the forgiveness of sins.[85]

In his teaching on the *Apostles Creed*, Martin
Luther set forth the forgiveness of sins as central to
Christ's Church. It was in the Church, Luther said, that
the treasure of the gospel was to be found and joyfully
received:

> Therefore everything in this Christian community is
> so ordered that everyone may daily obtain the for-
> giveness of sins through the Word and signs [baptism
> and the Lord's Supper] appointed to comfort and
> encourage our consciences as long as we live on earth.
> Although we have sin, the Holy Spirit sees to it that it
> does not harm us because we are part of the Christian
> community. Here there is full forgiveness of sins,
> both in that God forgives us and that we forgive, bear
> with, and aid one another.[86]

Each Lord's Day, Christ, the Bread of Life, is to be
freely offered through the preaching of the gospel for the
forgiveness of sins. Through the forgiveness of sins the
Christian is sanctified: "[God] imparts, increases, and
strengthens faith through the same Word [the preached
Word of the gospel] and the forgiveness of sins."[87] Thus,
preaching is not so much a matter of training people for
spiritual heroics. Rather, for Luther, preaching offers
weak and sinful people what they truly need: Christ.
Preaching also includes proclaiming God's law so that a
church may be first humbled and then filled with joy in
believing the gospel as a result. Then, as men, women, and
children return home with Christ alone in their hearts,
they go out rejoicing and advanced in their sanctification.

Who Are the Members of Christ's Church?

Forgiven sinners. First, Luther noted that Christ's Church is made up of *forgiven* sinners, for the Christian's need for forgiveness is ongoing until he gets to heaven. "Now, however, we remain only halfway pure and holy. The Holy Spirit must always work in us through the Word, granting us daily forgiveness until we attain to that life where there will be no more forgiveness."[88] Because of his constant need for forgiveness, the Christian must hear the gospel continually throughout his pilgrimage in this life. *Simul iustus et peccator*—at the same time just and a sinner—is a precious truth that comforts and encourages the child of God, freeing one to grow in faith and obedience without fear of condemnation.

Weak sinners. Second, Christ's Church is made up of *weak* sinners. Luther said that Christ himself came to earth in weakness to be with us in our frailty and helplessness: "We must be weak, and are willing to be in order that Christ's strength may dwell in us; as Saint Paul says, 'Christ's strength is made perfect in weakness.'"[89] When we see something of our weakness, we may wonder if Christ might reject us. Thus we may run from Christ when we realize our own frailty. Yet no matter how weak we find ourselves to be, Christ, the crucified Lamb, was weaker still. As the risen King and chief Shepherd, he carries us in our frailty all the days of our earthly pilgrimage.

Ordinary sinners. Finally, Christ's Church is made up of *ordinary* sinners. Having been justified by faith alone, we ordinary sinners must say farewell to hyper-spirituality and embrace obedience in plain, everyday life. Luther noticed that when we do not believe the gospel, we come up with our own standard of what constitutes true godliness. When this happens the glitter, hype, and expectation of our "extraordinary" works become added to the gospel message. Man comes up with his own system of holiness, forsaking the "ordinary" commandments of God. Without the gospel, we set out to impress one another with our spiritual sacrifice. Our neighbors may be impressed, but God will not:

> Those other deeds [spectacular deeds done to earn favor and to impress] captivate all eyes and ears. Aided by great splendor, expense, and magnificent buildings, they are so adorned that everything gleams and glitters… For when a priest stands in a golden [cloak], or a layperson spends a whole day in the church on his or her knees, that is considered a precious work that cannot be sufficiently extolled. But when a poor servant girl takes care of a little child or faithfully does what she is told, this is regarded as nothing.[90]

Because of the gospel of grace, Luther taught that all vocations are callings from God. To be an ordinary gardener is just as holy as being a missionary: both serve their neighbor and both are important. Our vocation, whatever it may be, is the theatre in which the fruit of the gospel is displayed. The centrality of the gospel and the forgiveness of sins inform our doctrine of vocation and bring beauty to all areas of society.

+ + +

We are soon approaching the five-hundredth anniversary of Luther's nailing of the ninety-five theses to the church door at Wittenberg. Despite all the time that has passed since that October day, we still face the same issues Luther did. Professing Christians in our day still desperately need a clear and accurate understanding of the biblical gospel—specifically, justification by faith alone and a clear distinction between God's law and God's gospel. Moreover, much of the Church is still influenced by many false gods, and therefore characterized by various forms of futile hyper-spirituality.

Yet is still also true that Luther's teaching, drawn plainly and directly from the Scriptures—the teaching that there is only one true and living God—this provides assurance and peace. This is the God of promise who comes to sinners by sheer grace. Luther's teaching that our wills are bound and that we are dependent on our gracious God for all things can once again produce a humble and holy people.

How desperately we need for God's majesty—having been eclipsed by our foolish wisdom—to once again be faithfully proclaimed and known through Luther's theology of the cross. How badly we need a worldwide revival of the law of God once again being preached in all its purity, majesty, and holiness, that we may once again see that we are truly sinners who have no hiding place besides Christ.

The Church is the glorious Body of Christ. We are forgiven, helpless, weak, and ordinary sinners who are daily being shaped by God's forgiveness and tender care in the midst of our weakness and frailty. Jesus is magnified in us. The gospel of God is our treasure—a treasure we alone possess, and a treasure that we must share with the whole world. The Church is to walk joyfully and humbly with God in weakness and need, Christ carrying us in our helplessness and failure, yet sanctifying us through forgiveness until we are home with him forever. Let us once again believe the gospel, and in so believing, joyfully share a single passion: Christ Jesus, the Lord of Glory, the friend of sinners.

As I come to the end of these essays and reflect on what has been written, I realize that Martin Luther's life and teaching have become something of an exposition of 1 Corinthians 1:18–31. Therefore, I can think of no better way to end than by simply sharing these beautiful words given to us from God himself:

> *For the word of the cross is foolishness to those who are perishing, but to us who are being saved it is the power of God. For it is written,*
>
> > *I will destroy the wisdom of the wise,*
> > *And the cleverness of the clever I will set aside.*
> > *Where is the wise man? Where is the scribe?*
>
> *Where is the debater of this age? Has not God made foolish the wisdom of the world? For since in the wisdom of God the world through its wisdom did not come to know God, God was well-pleased through the foolishness of the message preached to save those who believe. For indeed Jews ask for signs and Greeks search for wisdom; but we preach Christ crucified, to Jews a stumbling block and to Gentiles foolishness, but to those who are the called, both Jews and*

Greeks, Christ the power of God and the wisdom of God. Because the foolishness of God is wiser than men, and the weakness of God is stronger than men.

For consider your calling, brethren, that there were not many wise according to the flesh, not many mighty, not many noble; but God has chosen the foolish things of the world to shame the wise, and God has chosen the weak things of the world to shame the things which are strong, and the base things of the world and the despised God has chosen, the things that are not, so that he may nullify the things that are, so that no man may boast before God. But by his doing you are in Christ Jesus, who became to us wisdom from God, and righteousness and sanctification, and redemption, so that, just as it is written,

Let him who boasts, boast in the Lord.

1 Corinthians 1:18–31

APPENDIX

Simplified Timeline of Events Concerning Martin Luther's Life

1415	*July 6*	John Hus burned at the stake, c. 100 years before the Reformation
1483	*November 10*	Martin Luther born in Eisleben, Germany
1505		Begins study of Law
1505	*July 2*	Vows to become monk after thunderstorm
1505	*July 17*	Enters Augustinian order to become a monk
1507		Luther conducts his first Mass
1511		Transferred by Staupitz to Wittenberg from Erfurt
1513–1516		Lectures on Psalms, Romans, and Galatians at University of Wittenberg
1517	*October 31*	Announces 95 Theses in Wittenberg

1518	*April 26*	*Heidelberg Disputation*
1519	*July 4–14*	Debates Eck at Leipzig, *Sola Scriptura* is realized by Luther
1520		*Treatise on Good Works*, *To the Christian Nobility*, *The Babylonian Captivity of the Church*, and *The Freedom of the Christian* are published
1520		Pope Leo X issues papal bull giving Luther 60 days to recant
1521	*April 16–26*	Luther defends at the Diet of Worms
1521	*May 4*	Luther is hidden at the Wartburg castle
1522		Luther's German translation of the New Testament published
1524		Peasants' War begins. Thomas Munzer, a key leader of the Anabaptists
1525	*January 21*	Formal beginning of Anabaptist movement (Conrad Grebel baptizes)
1525		Luther marries Katherine Von Bora, a nun
1529		Marburg Colloquy (Luther & Zwingli split over the Lord's Supper)

1529		Luther writes *Large Catechism* (April) and *Small Catechism* (May)
1530	*June 25*	The Augsburg Confession is presented
1535		*Lectures on Galatians* is published
1536–1537		Luther writes Smalcald Articles
1539		Luther writes *Against the Antinomians*
1546	*February 18*	Martin Luther dies at age 62 in Eisleben, Germany

AUTHOR

Charles E. Fry (BA, Marshall University; BA, Moody Bible Institute) is currently pursuing an MA in Theology at Christ College, Irvine, where he enjoys studying the theology of the Reformation. He has taught several church history classes with the goal of sharing a high view of God and a clear understanding of the gospel. In 2011, Chuck was licensed for the ministry through the Baptist church.

Chuck is on staff with The Navigators in Huntington, West Virginia, and has been in discipleship ministry since 1989. He and his wife, Lisa, organize and host the annual Majesty of God Conference, held each April.

ACKNOWLEDGEMENTS

The author wishes to thank Cruciform Press for their kindness in editing and publishing this book. Thank you as well to Bill Walsh for reading the manuscript and for his endorsement. I am also very grateful for my dear brothers and sisters in Christ who read this manuscript and gave invaluable suggestions, loving criticism, and significant encouragement. In particular, I wish to thank Lisa, Nat and Debbie DeBruin, Daniel and Kim Hirmas, Bryan Barnett, and Josh Bailey. Thank you for your love for Christ and your simple trust in the gospel.

I especially want to thank C. FitzSimons Allison and John V. Fesko for the godly example of their lives and their uncluttered faithfulness to the doctrine of justification by faith alone.

Endnotes

1. James M. Kittelson, *Luther the Reformer: The Story of the Man and His Career* (Minneapolis: Fortress Press, 1986, 2003), 297.
2. *Sermons*, vol. 5, 11.
3. *Galatians*, 16.
4. Heiko A. Oberman, *Luther: Man Caught between God and the Devil* (New Haven: Yale, 1982, 1989, 2006), p. 26.
5. Lewis W. Spitz, *The Renaissance and Reformation Movements, volume 1* (St. Louis: Concordia Publishing, 1971, 1987), 17. Used with permission.
6. Thomas M. Lindsay, *A History of the Reformation: The Reformation in Germany*, (New York: Charles Scribner's Sons, 1916), 57.
7. Roland Bainton, *Here I Stand; A Life of Martin Luther* (Peabody, MA: Hendrickson, 1950, 1977, 2010), 53.
8   Frederick the Wise was deeply respected by Luther and would later become Luther's great protector. Frederick changed his view of relics and died a friend of the Reformation, believing in justification by faith alone.
9. *Galatians*, 156, 157.
10. Bainton, 41.
11. Kittelson, 134.
12. Bainton, 48. Emphasis added.
13. There is some scholarly discussion as to whether Luther actually nailed the 95 Theses to the church door at Wittenberg. The most contemporary accounts do not mention the door. There is only one mention of Luther nailing the theses to the door, and this account (by Melanchthon) was written many years after 1517. However, for the sake of familiarity, I have kept the traditional account in this book. I am indebted to Dr. Timothy Dost, church history professor at Concordia Seminary, St. Louis, for this observation. Class notes, Reformation History, Spring, 2015.
14. This important work is discussed in more detail in chapter three.
15. Bainton, 93, 97.
16. Ibid., p. 105. By "heretic," Luther was referring to John Hus or others who the Roman Catholic Church considered to be a heretic.
17. The famous phrase, "Here I stand; I can do no other," is disputed as to whether or not it was part of Luther's original words.
18. *Sermons*, vol. 5, 11.
19. *Galatians*, 16.

20. Philip Schaff, *History of the Christian Church, volume 7,The German Reformation* (Peabody, MA: Hendrickson, 1888, 2011), 341.

21. Robert Kolb, *Luther and the Stories of God: Biblical Narratives as a Foundation for Christian Living* (Grand Rapids, Baker Academic, 2012), 9.

22. Martin Luther, *The Second Sermon, March 10, 1522, Monday after Invocaviti*, in *Luther's Works, vol. 51* (Philadelphia: Fortress Press, 1959), 77, 78.

23. Martin Luther, *Sermon on the Afternoon of Christmas Day*, in *Martin Luther's Basic Theological Writings*, second edition, edited byTimothy F. Lull, (Minneapolis, MN., Fortress Press, 2005), 199.

24. Oberman, 3.

25. Ibid., 8.

26. Bainton, 13, 14.The quote is from Martin Luther.

27. While other primary sources are used for this chapter, the main reference used is Luther's *Lectures on Galatians* published in 1535 (Middleton version, Logos Bible Software).This work was done later in Luther's life and thus reflects his developed thought concerning the gospel. He said of this edition, "But since I recognise as mine all the thoughts which the brethren have taken such pains to set down in it, I am forced to admit that I said as much and perhaps even more." (Preface to 1535 publication of *Lectures on Galatians*, 16).

28. Martin Luther, "The Distinction between the Law and Gospel," January 1, 1532,Willard Burce, translator, *Concordia Journal* 18 (April 1992), 153.

29. Ibid., 156.

30. Ibid., 157. Emphasis added.

31. *Galatians*, 151.

32. Ibid., 152.

33. Ibid., 153.

34. Ibid., 131, 132.

35. *Festival of Christ's Nativity, Fifth Sermon*, December 27, 1532, *Sermons*, vol. 7, 251.

36. Philip S.Watson, *Let God be God*, (Philadelphia, Fortress Press, 1947, 1966), 21.

37. *Galatians*, 26.

38. Bainton, 48.

39. *Galatians*, 117.

40. Ibid., 227.

41. Ibid., 138.

42. Bainton, 71.
43. Martin Luther, "Smalcald Articles," found in *Concord*, 315.
44. *Concord*, 318.
45. *Sermons*, vol. 1.2, 149.
46. The Roman Catholic Church placed sins in one of two categories: 1. Mortal sin (mentioned above) or 2. Venial sin, which could be forgiven by works of merit.
47. Kittelson, 147.
48. Bainton, 48.
49. J.I. Packer and O.R. Johnston (eds.), *Martin Luther, The Bondage of the Will* 1525 (Westwood, NJ: Fleming Revell, 1957), 41.
50. *On the Bondage of the Will*, 87.
51. Ibid., 100.
52. Ibid., 101.
53. Luther used this phrase in at least two different places in his commentary on Galatians.
54. *Galatians*, 225, 226.
55. Thomas Watson, *The Ten Commandments* (Edinburgh: Banner of Truth, 1692, 1995), 186, parenthesis added.
56. A.A. Hodge, *Outlines in Theology* (Edinburgh: Banner of Truth, 1860, 1999), 539.
57. Benjamin Breckenridge Warfield, *"Miserable-Sinner Christianity" in the Hands of the Rationalists*, Article 1, found in, *The Works of Benjamin B. Warfield*, volume 7 (Grand Rapids: Baker, 1932, 2003), 113.
58. Ibid., 114.
59. Jerry Bridges, *The Practice of Godliness* (Colorado Springs: NavPress, 1983), 31.
60. Ibid., 33, 34.
61. Quoted in W. Robert Godfrey's essay, *Faith Formed by Love or Faith Alone? The Instrument of Justification*, in R. Scott Clark (ed.), *Covenant, Justification, and Pastoral Ministry* (Phillipsburg, NJ: Presbyterian and Reformed Publishing, 2007), 268.
62. Herman Bavinck, *Reformed Dogmatics*, vol. 1, John Bolt (ed.), John Vriend, translator (Grand Rapids: Baker Academic, 2003), 160.
63. The Wesleys were not always consistent with their understanding of justification they learned from Luther's commentaries at the beginning of their Christian life. Yet God used Luther to bring them to trust Christ alone for salvation.
64. Found in Bainton, 358.
65. *Festival of Christ's Nativity, Fifth Sunday*, December 27, 1532, in *Sermons*, 247.

66. W. Robert Godfrey, *Reformation Sketches* (Phillipsburg, NJ: P&R Publishing, 2003), 12, 13.
67. The version of *The Heidelberg Disputation* used for this chapter is found in Gerhard O. Forde, *On Being a Theologian of the Cross: Reflections on Luther's Heidelberg Disputation*, 1518 (Grand Rapids: Eerdmans), 1997.
68. Quoted in Forde, 39, 40.
69. The content of this chart is from personal study of *The Heidelberg Disputation*, along with reading Forde's *On Being a Theologian of the Cross*, and the last comparison from hearing a message by Carl Trueman, *The Theology of the Cross*, given at Grace Presbyterian Church's *Reformation Heritage Lectures series, 2007*, Douglasville, Georgia.
70. *Galatians*, 70.
71. Ibid., 132.
72. Ibid., 77.
73. Ibid., 21.
74. Ibid., 138.
75. Martin Luther, *On Christian Liberty (The Freedom of the Christian)*, (Minneapolis: Fortress Press, 1520, 2003), 2.
76. Ibid., 16.
77. Ibid., 32.
78. Ibid., 35.
79. Ibid., 39, 40.
80. Martin Luther, *Against the Antinomians*, in *Martin Luther's Basic Theological Writings*, Timothy F. Lull, ed., (Minneapolis: Fortress Press, 2005), 204.
81. Ibid., 205.
82. Ibid., 206.
83. Ibid., 203, emphases added.
84. *On Christian Liberty*, 33.
85. Philip S. Watson, *Let God be God*, (Philadelphia: Fortress Press, 1947, 1966), 26. Also B.A. Gerrish, *Grace and Reason: A Study in the Theology of Luther* (Eugene, Oregon: Wipf and Stock, originally published in 1962), 8, fn.2, 58.
86. *Concord*, 438.
87. Ibid., 439.
88. Ibid., 438.
89. Found in Theodore Tappert (editor and translator), *Luther's Letters of Spiritual Counsel* (Philadelphia: Westminster Press, 1960, and Vancouver: Regent College Publishing, 2003), 98.
90. *Concord*, 428.

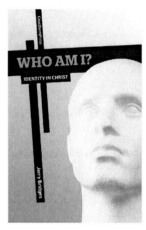

Who Am I?
Identity in Christ

by Jerry Bridges

Jerry Bridges unpacks Scripture to give the Christian eight clear, simple, interlocking answers to one of the most essential questions of life.

91 pages
bit.ly/WHOAMI

"Jerry Bridges' gift for simple but deep spiritual communication is fully displayed in this warm-hearted, biblical spelling out of the Christian's true identity in Christ."

J.I. Packer, Theological Editor, ESV Study Bible; author, Knowing God, A Quest for Godliness, Concise Theology

"I know of no one better prepared than Jerry Bridges to write *Who Am I?* He is a man who knows who he is in Christ and he helps us to see succinctly and clearly who we are to be. Thank you for another gift to the Church of your wisdom and insight in this book."

R.C. Sproul, founder, chairman, president, Ligonier Ministries; executive editor, Tabletalk magazine; general editor, The Reformation Study Bible

"*Who Am I?* answers one of the most pressing questions of our time in clear gospel categories straight from the Bible. This little book is a great resource to ground new believers and remind all of us of what God has made us through faith in Jesus. Thank the Lord for Jerry Bridges, who continues to provide the warm, clear, and biblically balanced teaching that has made him so beloved to this generation of Christians."

Richard D. Phillips, Senior Minister, Second Presbyterian Church, Greenville, SC

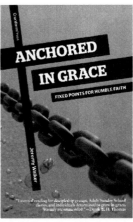

Anchored in Grace
Fixed Truths for Humble Faith

by Jeremy Walker

Clear truths from Scripture...

**Central. Humbling. Saving.
Comforting. God-glorifying.**

Get Anchored.

86 pages
bit.ly/ANCHRD

"Rarely does the title of a book so clearly represent its contents as does this one. With brevity and precision, Jeremy Walker sets forth God's work of salvation in the believer from beginning to end. In a day when there is so much confusion regarding even the most fundamental truths of redemption, this concise yet comprehensive work is a clear beacon of light to guide the seeker and to instruct and comfort the believer."
Paul David Washer, Director, HeartCry Missionary Society

"As a pastor, I am always looking for a book that is brief, simple, and biblical in its presentation of the God-exalting doctrines of grace to put into the hands of believers. I think my search is now over!"
Conrad Mbewe, African Christian University, Lusaka, Zambia

"Crisp, clear, concise, and biblical, Walker's book offers up the doctrines of God's grace in a manner persuasive to the mind and powerful to the heart."
Dr. Joel R. Beeke, Pres., Puritan Reformed Theological Seminary

"A sure-footed journey...a trusted guide. Reading this book will both thrill and convict, challenge and confirm. Essential reading for discipleship groups, Adult Sunday School classes, and individuals determined to grow in grace. Warmly recommended."
Derek W. H. Thomas, Professor, Reformed Theological Seminary

Inductive Bible Studies for Women by Keri Folmar

JOY! – A Bible Study on Philippians for Women

bit.ly/JoyStudy

GRACE: A Bible Study on Ephesians for Women

bit.ly/GraceStudy

FAITH: A Bible Study on James for Women

bit.ly/FaithStudy

"It is hard to imagine a better inductive Bible Study tool."
–Diane Schreiner

Keri's studies have been endorsed by...

Kathleen Nielson is author of the *Living Word Bible Studies;* Director of Women's Initiatives, The Gospel Coalition; and wife of Niel, who served as President of Covenant College from 2002 to 2012.

Diane Schreiner – wife of professor, author, and pastor Tom Schreiner, and mother of four grown children – has led women's Bible studies for more than 20 years.

Connie Dever is author of *The Praise Factory* children's ministry curriculum and wife of Pastor Mark Dever, President of 9 Marks Ministries.

Kristie Anyabwile, holds a history degree from NC State University, and is married to Thabiti, currently a church planter in Washington, D.C., and a Council Member for The Gospel Coalition.

Gloria Furman is a pastor's wife in the Middle East and author of *Glimpses of Grace* and *Treasuring Christ When Your Hands Are Full.*

Licensed to Kill
A Field Manual for Mortifying Sin

by Brian G. Hedges

Your soul is a war zone.

Know your enemy.

Learn to fight.

101 pages
bit.ly/L2Kill

"Are there things you hate that you end up doing anyway? Have you tried to stop sinning in certain areas of your life, only to face defeat over and over again? If you're ready to get serious about sin patterns in your life—ready to put sin to death instead of trying to manage it—this book outlines the only strategy that works. This is a book I will return to and regularly recommend to others."
Bob Lepine, Co-Host, **FamilyLife Today**

"Rather than aiming at simple moral reformation, *Licensed to Kill* aims at our spiritual transformation. Like any good field manual, this one focuses on the most critical information regarding our enemy, and gives practical instruction concerning the stalking and killing of sin. This is a theologically solid and helpfully illustrated book that holds out the gospel confidence of sin's ultimate demise."
Joe Thorn, pastor and author, **Note to Self: The Discipline of Preaching to Yourself**

"Read this 'field-manual' and you will discover that you have a monstrous and aggressive antagonist who is aiming to annihilate you. It's your duty to fight back! Brian has given us a faithful, smart, Word-centered guide to help us identify and form a battle plan for mortally wounding the enemy of indwelling sin."
Wes Ward, Revive Our Hearts

"But God..."
The Two Words at the Heart of the Gospel

by Casey Lute

Just two words.
Understand their use in Scripture,
and you will never be the same.

100 pages
bit.ly/ButGOD

"Keying off of nine occurrences of "But God" in the English Bible, Casey Lute ably opens up Scripture in a manner that is instructive, edifying, encouraging, and convicting. This little book would be useful in family or personal reading, or as a gift to a friend. You will enjoy Casey's style, you will have a fresh view of some critical Scripture, and your appreciation for God's mighty grace will be deepened."
Dan Phillips, Pyromaniacs blog, author of The World-Tilting
Gospel (forthcoming from Kregel)

"A refreshingly concise, yet comprehensive biblical theology of grace that left this reader more in awe of the grace of God."
Aaron Armstrong, BloggingTheologically.com

""Casey Lute reminds us that nothing is impossible with God, that we must always reckon with God, and that God brings life out of death and joy out of sorrow."
Thomas R. Schreiner, Professor of New Testament
Interpretation, The Southern Baptist Theological Seminary

"A mini-theology that will speak to the needs of every reader of this small but powerful book. Read it yourself and you will be blessed. Give it to a friend and you will be a blessing."
William Varner, Prof. of Biblical Studies, The Master's College

CPSIA information can be obtained at www.ICGtesting.com
Printed in the USA
BVOW02s1903210915

418991BV00004B/4/P